Shoeless

Shoeless

Carmelite Spirituality in a Disquieted World

Donald *and* Megan
Wallenfang

WIPF & STOCK · Eugene, Oregon

Wipf & Stock
An Imprint of Wipf and Stock Publishers
199 W. 8th Ave., Suite 3
Eugene, OR 97401

www.wipfandstock.com

PAPERBACK ISBN: 978-1-6667-0003-9
HARDCOVER ISBN: 978-1-6667-0004-6
EBOOK ISBN: 978-1-6667-0005-3

08/16/21

To our Mother and Father in Shoeless Carmel,
Saint Teresa of Jesus and Saint John of the Cross

קַנֹּא קִנֵּאתִי לַיהוָה אֱלֹהֵי צְבָאוֹת
Zelo zelatus sum pro Domino Deo exercituum.
1 Kgs 19:10, 14

Contents

Introduction

BORN ON JULY 16, 1887, in Pickens County, South Carolina, Joseph Jefferson Jackson was destined to become a world-class Major League Baseball player. At the pinnacle of his playing career, he would help lead the Chicago White Sox to a World Series title against the New York Giants in 1917, amidst the din of World War I. Before ascending to these great heights, however, he had to pay his dues. Early on, he played in the Minor League for the Greenville Spinners. During his first year in the minors, at the tender age of nineteen, he began to develop blisters on his feet from his new baseball shoes. He was confined to the dugout to heal, but game day came and his team was short of players. His coach called upon him to bat and, instead of wearing his new cleats, he stepped up to home plate in his bare stockings. It was the seventh inning. He proceeded to hit a triple and, when sliding into third base, a fan called out from the stands nearby: "You shoeless son-of-a-gun, you!" From that day on, he was nicknamed "Shoeless" Joe Jackson.

And so it is with the spiritual life. On our route toward intimacy with God, we must pay our dues; we must bide our time; we must suffer humiliation and then discover the divinely orchestrated meaning in it. As yet another exercise in humiliation, I want to invite you to do something unusual while you read this book in the comfort of wherever you are. Take off your shoes. That's right. Go ahead, take 'em off. Take off your socks as well. Now, how does it feel? Exposure. Nakedness. Vulnerability. Exactly. This is the essence of Carmelite spirituality, and, in particular, that of Discalced Carmelite spirituality in the Teresian tradition. For the word "discalced" means "shoeless" or "barefoot" and it symbolizes a way of life akin to the greatest prophets in human history: Elijah the Tishbite, Ezekiel the Exiled Priest, Mary the Virgin Mother, John the Baptist, Mary of Egypt, Teresa of Jesus, Teresa Benedicta of the Cross. These prophets were attuned acutely to their surrounding environment and their role within it, just as naked feet are attuned to the immediate world around them. The spiritual meaning of naked feet extends with rich textures throughout the whole of Scripture. First, there is the humble act of washing the feet of one's guests. We observe this scene with Abraham's invitation to his three divine passersby (Gen 18:4), with Lot as host to two angelic personas (Gen 19:2), with Rebekah's welcome of Abraham's servant (Gen 24:32), with Joseph's hospitality toward his brothers (Gen 43:24), with Jesus and his stupefied disciples (John 13:1–20). Moreover, we encounter with surprise the humble wife-to-be of King David, Abigail, whose name means "my Father's joy" or "my Father is joy," a self-identified "maidservant" who vows to be "the slave who washes the feet of my lord's servants" (Gen 25:41).

Removing one's footwear is a premier sign of gratitude in response to the divine Host who desires to wash our feet. As Jesus solemnly declares to Peter: "Unless I wash you, you will have no inheritance with me" (John 13:8). To shed one's shoes implies the ultimate degree of spiritual humility and submission to the divine will. It signifies proximity to the holy. Recall Moses's encounter with the mysterious inbreaking of divine Presence in the phenomenon of a bush engulfed in flames yet not consumed: "Do not come near! Remove your sandals from your feet, for the place where you stand is holy ground" (Exod 3:5). Again, remember Joshua's encounter with the angelic military figure on the eve of the siege at Jericho: "Remove your sandals from your feet, for the place on which you are standing is holy" (Josh 5:15). Naked feet mirror nakedness of the will before God. It's like saying to God, "Here are my feet, Lord, naked before you. Tell me where you want them to go." After all, the whole body is supported by the feet, and the feet are the means by which the entire body moves toward its goal of action and purpose. Feet are foundation. We call ourselves "pedestrians" because we travel by foot (Latin: *pes*) and our feet are our primary mode of transportation. Even when our feet are broken or disabled, this occasion empowers another's feet to come to our assistance. And this, too, inaugurates an event of grace.

Second, going about barefoot is an indication of poverty, repentance, and mission. Several allusions throughout Scripture make this clear. Following the conspiracy of his son Absalom against him, David ascended the Mount of Olives, weeping with head covered and feet exposed (see 2 Sam 15:30). Serving as a sign and portent against Egypt and Ethiopia, God instructed the prophet Isaiah to go about naked and barefoot for three years (see Isa 20:1–6). Micah, likewise, in his prophetic office, goes about naked and barefoot, uttering mourning and lamentation for the sins of the Judahites (see Mic 1:8). Upon commissioning his apostles to proclaim the kingdom of heaven to the Jewish people, Jesus directs them not to wear sandals (see Matt 10:10; Luke 10:4). Historically, it has been common for prisoners and slaves to be compelled to live shoeless. Across cultures, to appear shoeless is a sign of reverence and submission to the authority of another. It implies piety and obedience, as well as humiliation. Similarly, living in poverty may preclude the possibility of affording footwear, thereby eliciting the connotation of being in want. This is the meaning of repentance: to be in want of forgiveness and grace. And this is the meaning of mission: to be thrown, sent, propelled, launched, or hurled on your way. A shoeless mission refers to its urgency, seriousness, and boldness. It's as if to suggest that there is nothing more important than the mission itself.

It is also apropos that, in Hebrew idiom, the notion of uncovered feet is a euphemism for the sexual faculties, and to cover one's feet signifies modesty and chastity. Take, for instance, the vision beheld by the prophet Isaiah: "I saw the Lord seated on a high and lofty throne, with the train of his garment filling the temple. Seraphim were stationed above; each of them had six wings: with two they covered their faces, with two they covered their feet, and with two they hovered" (Isa 6:1–2). Altogether we come to understand that feet symbolize both the power and the humility of the person. They connote the sexual splendor and vulnerability of the human person as male or female. Feet convey the universal human vocation to become a total gift of self to the other. As the lowest extremity of the body, it is the feet that are most familiar with the ground. They are accustomed to dust, to getting soiled, to becoming scuffed-up, bruised, and bothered. They are literally the lowest members of the body, acquainted with mud and muck. Yet it is the feet that lead the way in taking us to where we want to go. It is no coincidence that we read later in the book of Isaiah: "How beautiful upon the mountains are the feet of the one bringing good news, announcing peace, bearing good news, announcing salvation, saying to Zion, 'Your God is King!'" (Isa 52:7; cf. Rom 10:15). Our feet are beautiful because they remind us at once of our power and humility, especially when they are nailed to a cross of wood. Indeed, how beautiful it is that our God has feet.

Are you called to be a Discalced Carmelite, whether religious or secular? Well, it depends on how you feel about living "shoeless." This book is all about the life and charism of Carmel. It aims to be a primer of sorts for Carmelite spirituality, especially as lived out by the members of the Secular Order of Discalced Carmelites (*Ordo Carmelitarum Discalceatorum Saecularis*, or OCDS). It will mark out in brief the history of the order, the primary elements of its unique charism, the five stages of prayer according to Saint Teresa of Ávila, and the testimony of its authors. Before we turn to chapter 1 and its account of the history of the Discalced Carmelites, let us take a moment to come to terms with our contemporary cultural context of the early twenty-first century.

We are busy. This much is sure. While privileged with the latest technological advancements—the World Wide Web being one of the finest—we are inundated with information and virtual avatars of the real. This has become the backdrop of our contemporary metanarrative—our grand story. Fast food (now with at least two traffic lanes), mobile devices, frequent-flyer miles, Fitbits, and self-checkout lines are among the phenomena that pepper our daily lives. We've come a long way from the horse-and-buggy lifestyle in force only a century ago, save for the Amish communities and other cultural outliers who continue to witness to those invaluable human touchpoints that have become tragically lost on the rest of the world. With more so-called convenience comes more demands on our time. Have our lives become dictated by our own modes of convenience? Without doubt, they have. Yet we yearn for something else—something that is not to be found with a price tag or a promise on this side of eternity. Our very desires attest to the quench of the infinite and nothing less than the infinite. We are finite, limited, but we sense that our origin is not so. It cannot be. We are at least convinced that the source of it all is not identical to "it all." The source is that for which we thirst, and the thirst itself is evidence of the source. This source we call God, the divine, divinity. We yearn for God, and we know deep down that God alone satisfies all of our passions and desires. This is the beginning of the secret of Carmel. Jesus calls it "the pearl of great price," "the treasure hidden in a field," "the lost coin," "the seed," "the child," "salt," "leaven," "light." It is something small, yet the greatest of all gifts. It is something hidden, yet revealed for all to see. It is something ordinary, yet opens onto the most extraordinary meaningfulness of our experience.

The Hebrew word *carm-el* means "garden of God" or "paradise of God." It suggests an ecosystem of grace in which to serve is to reign. It engenders an imagination of wonder: countless flowers coexisting in their majestic display of color, fragrance, fertility, and bounty. A saturating unity in diversity. Perhaps the fine paradox of the flower's stunning radiant meekness and simple beauty lends itself to match the scandalous paradox of our human situation. The flower is so fragile, so precarious; nevertheless it pronounces an authoritative potency in the way it decorates the mute earth and turns to face the light. Majesty manifest in littleness. Humility (earth, soil) as the condition for the possibility of life's germination. It is the contemplative gaze of Carmel that grants one admission into the sacramental display of the cosmos. Saint Elizabeth of the Trinity puts it this way: "Each incident, each event, each suffering, as well as each joy, is a sacrament which gives God to it."[1] Through contemplative prayer the whole world lights up, and the possibility of its redemption comes into view. This is the meaning and purpose of sacrament. Carmel is a mission field of contemplation wherein "much will be required of the person entrusted with much, and still more will be demanded of the person entrusted with more" (Luke 12:48).

If you are attracted to this kind of contemplative vocation, if you are magnetized and persuaded by the lives of the Carmelite saints, if you are yearning for a pathway to intimacy with God, if you are groping for a way to connect your life of prayer with the redemption of the world, then the OCDS community could be your home. In it you will find a paradise of rest, a palace of encouragement, and a prime venue to challenge your hidden weaknesses. You will be brought into the company of witnesses on a journey like you, vulnerable like you, and earnest like you. Carmel is a verdant pasture of mercy—where all is turned to grace at the touch of the divine Shepherd, Pastor of souls, where sheep may safely graze, and where what was lost may be found.

---

1. Elizabeth of the Trinity, *Complete Works*, 1:97.

History

1

History of the Carmelite Movement

I. ELIJAH, THE ZEALOUS PROPHET

CARMELITE HISTORY BEGINS NEITHER in medieval times nor even in the post-apostolic period, but in the ancient Hebrew world with the prophet Elijah. Though some Carmelite lore would regard Elijah as the original founder of the Carmelite Order, a more modest historical reading considers Elijah to be the spiritual father of the religious movement toward eremitic life and contemplation. Why Elijah? Three classic scenes put us into contact with the distinct character of Elijah: the feeding of the widow and her son and the resuscitation of that widow's son (1 Kgs 17:7–24), the showdown with the false prophets of Baal on Mount Carmel (1 Kgs 18:1–46), and the flight to Mount Horeb, on which mount Elijah encounters the living God and appoints his successor, Elisha (1 Kgs 19:1–21). All three scenes demonstrate the virtue of faith: trusting in divine providence no matter what the circumstances. In the first scene, a famine has struck the land of Israel and beyond, and Elijah is led by the Spirit of God to go to the home of a widow and her son in Zarephath. Located about forty miles north of Mount Carmel and situated, like Mount Carmel, on the Mediterranean coast, Zarephath is an unusual point of destination for the Jewish prophet. It is in Sidon, that is, Gentile territory (see Luke 4:16–30). Overall, this story illustrates an inclusive summons to salvation and sounds overtones of the Eucharist and the future doctrine of resurrection as Elijah sustains the widow and her son's food supply and resuscitates the widow's son back to life.

In the second tale, Elijah confronts the false prophets of Baal who were leading the Israelites away from the one true God. In dramatic fashion, Elijah's word is vindicated and he puts to death all the false prophets of Baal with the sword. Why such a severe sentence? Because this is the seriousness and soberness between life and death, between truth and falsehood. It is better to die than to live as a false witness. It is significant that this episode takes place on Mount Carmel—separating the true God (Hebrew: *El*) from the false one. Elijah's zeal for truth, for justice, and for the living God is shown here.

In the third passage, related sequentially to the heels of the previous one, Elijah is fleeing his death threat from the evil Queen Jezebel. It is in his agony, torment, and desperately lonely solitude that Elijah once again encounters the providence of the living God. He takes shelter in a cave, setting the precedent and model for the eremitic life, and there encounters God like never before: not in the strong and violent wind, not in the earthquake, not in the blazing fire, but in a small whispering voice. קוֹל דְּמָמָה דַקָּה A tiny, light, quiet sound. Upon this silent locution, Elijah hides his face and is addressed by God: "Why are you here, Elijah?" Elijah's response?

קַנֹּא קִנֵּאתִי לַיהוָה אֱלֹהֵי צְבָאוֹת
Zelo zelatus sum pro Domino Deo exercituum.
"I have been most zealous for the LORD, the God of hosts."
1 Kgs 19:14

With this utterance of Elijah, we arrive at the heart of the Carmelite tradition: zeal for the LORD God of hosts. This zeal is an impassioned and ardent desire to seek and to find the living God. However, in these narratives about Elijah and his pursuit of God, another wonderful mystery is revealed: this God whom Elijah pursues has been pursuing Elijah all along. At a certain point, the one who chooses God realizes that he has been chosen by God ahead of time. Yes, quite literally, ahead of time—before time began, in God's eternal "time" of love. Prevenient election and grace.

II. MARY, MOTHER OF GOD, AND JOHN THE BAPTIST

About nine hundred years later, in "the fullness of time," amidst the hill country of Judea, two women and their infants embraced, enveloped in the promises of God: Mary and Elizabeth, Jesus and John the Baptist. We are brought to two other important instigators of the Carmelite way of life:

Mary, mother of Jesus, and John the Baptist, the return of Elijah's persona (see Mal 3:22–24; Matt 11:14; 17:10–13; Mark 9:11–13) to prepare the way of the Lord. Like Elijah, Mary and John bear the mystical and prophetic zeal of individuals set on doing God's will. In Mary's case, her zeal is interior and incarnate and takes the form of manifestation. In John's case, his zeal is announced and enacted externally in his ministry of ritual baptism and takes the form of proclamation. With Mary, the Word becomes flesh, and with John, a way is prepared for this Word to be heard in the wilderness of humanity. According to the textual witness of Luke's Gospel, Mary "kept all these things, reflecting on them in her heart" (Luke 2:19, 51). In other words, Mary ponders with great restful intensity the mysteries of God unfolding in her life and for the life of the world. For John's part, he offers a legacy of self-denial and self-forgetfulness that will become a hallmark of Carmelite spirituality: "He must increase; I must decrease" (John 3:30).

A third key historical moment that would lead to the Carmelite movement, besides that of the time of Elijah and the fullness of time featuring Mary and John the Baptist, is the developing era of the desert hermits. Derived from the Greek words *eremos* (desolate, lonely) and *eremia* (desert), a hermit—also referred to as an anchorite, recluse, or monk—is someone who withdraws from organized human society into a solitary place, such as the desert, for concentrated prayer, fasting and penance. The word desert is derived from a negation of the Latin verb *serere* (to join together), altogether meaning to pull apart or to detach. A hermit sets out on the course toward solitude and radical poverty in order to detach himself from structures of sin and vice that tend to run rampant in human society and that often infest the soul. The desert is the perfect place for this detox to happen, and the purpose of an eremitic life is salvation. It is for the all-consuming love of God that a man or woman would leave everything behind to seek the face of the living God, day and night, with very little distraction.

III. THE DESERT HERMITS AND THE RISE OF MONASTICISM

Collectively known as the Desert Fathers and Mothers, the eremitic way of life traces its origins back to figures such as Elijah and John the Baptist, and even Simeon and Anna (see Luke 2:25–38), but assumes a more definitive historical shape with the lives of Paul of Thebes (died ca. 341), Antony of Egypt (ca. 251–356), Pachomius of Egypt (292–348), Syncletica of Alexandria (died ca. 350), Basil of Caesarea (330–379), and their successors. These were the spiritual athletes of the early church. They set the model for the most rigorous form of Christian discipleship possible. Renouncing all that the world had to offer, the desert hermits gave up everything for the sake of Christ and to follow him out into the unknown recesses of arid wilderness. According to the biographical account of Antony by Athanasius of Alexandria, Antony's eremitic conversion happened when he heard the passage from the Gospel of Matthew read at liturgy that said, "If you wish to be perfect, go, sell what you have and give to the poor, and you will have treasure in heaven. Then come, follow me" (Matt 19:21). Upon hearing these words, Antony did just that and gradually migrated all the way out into the desert terrain of the Natron Valley. There he would be nourished by date palms and desert springs. Periodically, friends would bring him bread and other basic necessities as well. With Pachomius came the formal organization of monastic communal life, including both men and women. Manual labor was a part of monasticism from its beginnings as a way to support the material needs of the community. A little later on, Basil of Caesarea and Augustine of Hippo (354–430) would write authoritative Rules to govern monastic life in community.

Fast forward about a century to the epiphany of Benedict of Nursia (480–543). Becoming an understudy of a seasoned hermit, Romanus of Subiaco (died ca. 550), Benedict was initiated into the eremitic way of life and would later found twelve monasteries in the Subiaco region and one on Monte Cassino. Benedict is referred to often as the father of Western monasticism. Even though the eremitic way of life was established centuries before his time, it was Benedict's rule that would set the golden standard for the monastic vocation in the Latin church for centuries to come. Adopting the motto *ora et labora* (prayer and work), the Benedictines approach monastic life with a sense of balance and stability, traditionally subdividing their time evenly between prayer, manual labor, and sleep. However, the commitment to live separately from the world would remain a defining characteristic of monastic life. The legacy of the hermits would live on in the organized monastic tradition of the Benedictines.

IV. NEW RELIGIOUS ORDERS AND THE MENDICANT WAY OF LIFE

Nearing the emergence of the Carmelite Order, let us jump ahead to the beginning of the thirteenth century and the creation of the great mendicant orders of the church: the Franciscans, Dominicans, Augustinians, and Servites. From the Latin verb *mendicare* (to beg), in contrast to monasticism, the mendicant orders were defined by transience, adaptability, and their commitment to missionary apostolates that tended to focus themselves in the growing urban areas with all of their needs and demands. In the High Middle Ages, more and more people were leaving the purely agrarian lifestyle and taking up residence in urban social centers. As Europe became more politically stable, universities and trade industries were developed and the economy soared. At the same time, the Crusades were well underway, in spite of their questionable intentions and outcomes, forming new cultural bridges between Europe and Arabia.

Instead of taking a vow of stability like the Benedictines, the mendicants adopted an itinerant way of life and devoted themselves to a variety of pastoral ministries, such as caring for the poor, homeless, uneducated, and infirm. They became university students and teachers, tending schools and transforming the culture from the inside out. Scholastic theology reached its zenith during the thirteenth century with the likes of the Dominican theologian Thomas Aquinas (1225–1274) and Bonaventure (1221–1274), the Italian Franciscan lecturer. Both studied and taught at the famed University of Paris. Living day in and day out within the academic sphere afforded new styles of spirituality and fresh approaches to theological questions. Scholasticism was only one outgrowth of mendicant religious life, alongside others such as Catholic hospitals, structured school systems for all ages, and enhanced parish life and ministry. Because the center of communal life for the mendicants shifted from a solitary abbey to geographically versatile priories and friaries located in urban sectors, mendicant friars lived in close proximity to people of all walks of life and were able to minister to them accordingly. However, a growing tension would develop between the competing demands of prayer and pastoral ministry. It was during this semi-stable era that the Carmelites appeared on the evolving landscape of religious life.

V. THE BIRTH OF THE CARMELITES

Just before the year 1200, the Brothers of the Most Blessed Virgin of Mount Carmel were established on the western slopes of Mount Carmel, overlooking the Mediterranean Sea. As tradition has it, the first Carmelites were laymen of the Latin military of the Third Crusade (1189–1192). Less certain are the identities of those men who founded the monastic community, but legend names the original founder and first superior as the French layman Berthold of Calabria. He is credited with directing the building of the first monastery and church in honor of the prophet Elijah. One testimony has it that Berthold was a soldier of the Crusader army and that he made a vow in battle under the walls of Antioch. He promised God that if he was delivered from the encroaching Turkish army, under the command of the ruler Zengi, he would found a monastery in the Holy Land. Berthold was spared in battle and followed through with his promise.

Tradition goes on to name Berthold's successor as Brother Brocard (died in 1231). Instead of adopting the Rule of Saint Basil, the Rule of Saint Augustine, or the Rule of Saint Benedict, the Carmelite Brothers petitioned the Patriarch of Jerusalem, Albert Avogadro, to compose for them their own unique Rule or *formula vitae*, that is, form of life. This Albert did sometime between 1206 and 1214. The Rule of Saint Albert was approved by Pope Honorius III in 1226. It is important to note that Albert was previously bishop of Vercelli and assumed the appointment as Patriarch of Jerusalem with its high probability of persecution and the likely prospect of martyrdom. Indeed, Albert was martyred while taking part in a procession on the feast of the Exaltation of the Holy Cross in 1214. The Carmelite charism is imbued with the vocation to martyrdom, through a daily life of sacrificial prayer, mortification, and self-denial, sharing in the redemptive power and witness of Christ crucified.

In contrast to the mendicant way of life, the original Carmelite community intended to return to the eremitic cast as set forth by the early Desert Fathers and Mothers. It was to be an Order dedicated to "meditating day and night on the Law of the Lord and watching in prayer" (Rule of Saint Albert). They understood themselves to be desert hermits, promising obedience, chastity, and poverty, holding all things in common. They were to give themselves over to silence and solitude for the salvation of souls, with each one assigned to a separate cell, in which or near which he was to remain for the greater part of the day. Not just out of fear of being sullied by worldly vice did these hermits withdraw from society in seclusion, but for the sake of their brethren, "to relate with God as with a friend . . . to walk in the presence of the living God (see 1 Kgs 18:14) . . . to know God that he may be known."[1] It was a life given over to penance and to vicarious prayer on behalf of the world. As much abandonment, so much redemption.

VI. CARMELITE MIGRATION AND REFORM

In 1238, political unrest and the threat of invasion forced the Carmelite community to migrate northwest to the island of Cyprus. Between 1241 and 1250, the Carmelites expanded to Sicily, England, Provence, and then throughout Europe during the latter half of the thirteenth century. It was at this time that the Carmelite Order faced an identity crisis. Would they remain faithful to their original charism of solitude, contemplation, and eremitic life, or would they be constrained to adapt to the missionary lifestyle of the mendicants? Practical pressures mounted, and, on the whole, the Carmelites were obliged to assume new apostolates and a more fluid vocational self-understanding. Subsequently, the Carmelite Rule was mitigated or revised according to the particular needs of their new social settings. As mendicants, they would need to seek support in habitable places, near or within the expanding urban centers, rather than reside exclusively in solitary locales. With a new mendicant way of life came new challenges for a communal charism inspired by the audacious model of the early desert hermits. The tale of frustration and dismay of this historical evolution from paradisiacal Mount Carmel to obsequious *praedium urbanum* (city land) is told by Carmelite Nicholas Gallicus in his *Ignea Sagitta* ("The Flaming Arrow," ca. 1270).[2] These challenges faced men and women alike as both the first institution of Carmelite nuns and the first Order of tertiaries were founded in 1452 under the leadership of Carmelite Prior General John Soreth. Expanding the Carmelite Order to include second- and third-order

---

1. General Definitory, *Constitutions*, 9, 17; Washington Province, *OCDS Provincial Statutes*, 25.

2. A similar point of tension was experienced by the first religious convent of women founded in the United States, the Discalced Carmelite community of Mount Carmel Monastery in Port Tobacco, Maryland, in 1790, under the warm approval of the first Catholic bishop of the United States, Bishop John Carroll. Soon after making the foundation, the Carmelite nuns were called upon to teach in a Catholic school—an experience which seemed to pull them away from their original vocation to contemplative prayer. See Liptak, "Living the Carmelite Mission."

members made a positive impact on the Carmelite family, as would be evidenced in the years to follow.

Two centuries later, compromise with the ways of the world would only escalate. Midway through the sixteenth century, a humble Spanish Carmelite nun named Teresa of Jesus grew convicted about how it became difficult to tell the difference between the monastery and the marketplace. Materialism, concern about proper manners and social etiquette, and excessive visitation overran the monastery, making it seem, at times, like just another center of religious coquetry. Thus began Teresa's courageous reform movement within the Carmelite community in an attempt to recuperate and restore the eremitic spirit of the penitential Desert Fathers and Mothers. In 1562, by divine grace and providence, Teresa of Jesus founded the first reformed monastery of the Carmelite Order, now known as the Order of Discalced Carmelites (OCD). In 1580, the OCD became a separate province and in 1593, it became an independent order by papal act. Teresa's reform was inspired by Saint Paul's injunction to "pray without ceasing" (1 Thess 5:17) and the yearning to return to the primitive Rule of Saint Albert.

Just a glance at Teresa's *Constitutions* for the Discalced Carmelites indicates the austerity, asceticism, and radical poverty demanded by the strict enclosure:

> Meat must never be eaten unless out of necessity as the rule prescribes. The habit should be made of coarse cloth or black, rough wool, and only as much wool as is necessary should be used . . . attending always to the necessary rather than the superfluous . . . . Straw-filled sacks will be used for mattresses . . . . Colored clothing or bedding must never be used, not even something as small as a ribbon . . . . The Sisters must keep their hair cut so as not to have to waste time in combing it. Never should a mirror be used or any adornments; there should be complete self-forgetfulness.[3]

This short sample from the *Constitutions* is enough to give a sense of the striking starkness of the strict enclosure "in order to observe the rule with greater perfection."[4] Highest degrees of penance, mortification, and detachment were to serve the itinerary of spiritual perfection and undivided union of the contemplative soul with God. Going about daily living with bare feet and fervent self-denial would characterize the reformed movement of the Teresian Carmel.

3. Teresa of Ávila, *Collected Works*, 3:322–23.
4. Teresa of Ávila, *Collected Works*, 1:321.

Today there are three main branches of the Carmelite family: the Order of Carmelites of the Ancient Observance (O. Carm.), including the tertiary order, the Third Order of Carmelites (T. O. Carm.); the Order of Discalced Carmelites (OCD), including the tertiary order, the Secular Order of Discalced Carmelites (OCDS); and the tertiary Order of the Carmelites of Mary Immaculate (CMI), a religious institute for men in the Syro-Malabar church, founded in 1831 in Kerala, India. The CMI community is more mendicant in nature, as it is involved in active evangelization and social work. It evolved largely as a result of the positive process of inculturation within the particular cultural milieu of India. In sum, the Carmelites are a diversified family sharing a common heritage and the primary vocation to contemplative prayer.

VII. FROM ELIJAH TO THE SECULAR ORDER OF DISCALCED CARMELITES

Beginning with the prophet Elijah and running through the reform movement of Teresa of Jesus up to the present time, we have examined the origin and evolution of the Carmelite Order in brief. Given this historical synopsis, we are able to understand the origin of the Order's variety of branches. Because this book is born from the experience of the Secular Order of Discalced Carmelites, we will shift our focus back to the identity and apostolate of the OCDS in several of the pages to follow. There are over 1,700 OCDS communities in seventy-five countries today, numbering over 25,000 members worldwide. Since their inception with the petition of John Soreth in 1452, the tertiary Carmelites have expanded to great proportion. It must be admitted at the outset, given the historical backdrop, that the meaning of a "secular Carmelite" is a paradox of sorts. How can a hermit live in the precincts of the secular? Or inversely, how can someone living in the hustle and bustle of secular life at the same time live as a contemplative hermit? Here is where we arrive at the wonderful reality of "the *hermitage of the heart*, where the living God is encountered," as Discalced Carmelite Steven Payne eloquently puts it.[5] To be explored in chapter 2, the mystery of the human soul—of every human soul—bears the potential to be a tabernacle of the Trinity—Father, Son, and Holy Spirit. If the desert hermits have taught us anything at all, it is that God does not desire to dwell in the desert, but in the precious spiritual chambers of the soul. However, we must often

5. Payne, *Carmelite Tradition*, xxxii.

take leave into the silent sand-swept solitude to rediscover that sanctuary where God is nearest.

This is the secret revealed in Carmel: that you are a child of God and, as a child, God's delightful dwelling place. You are a living cathedral. You are beloved by God. That is why you exist, why God loved you into being. This is the mystery of being of which the prophets were charged with alerting the world. This is the message proclaimed from the heights of Mount Carmel and echoed by all the Carmelite saints throughout history. This is the essence of the gospel and the chief meaning of the kingdom of God: you are beloved. As all the Carmelite saints give witness, the summit of Mount Carmel is union with God. We all yearn for this personal and communal union more than anything else, and Carmel provides a home in which to pursue this everlasting hunger of our souls. The Carmelite saints, with their lives and writings, serve as luminaries for the soul's movement toward divine union.

By recalling the history of the Carmelite Order, we have been reacquainted with its reason for being and with its most fundamental charism. In the chapters to follow, we will query the various elements and layers of this charism in order to live it out more constantly by God's grace. We will attempt to answer such questions as: What is meant by contemplative prayer? What is the nature of the soul and what does it mean to say that God dwells there? How do the Carmelite saints understand the virtue of humility, and how can one grow in humility? What is the relationship between the interior life and exterior apostolates of service? What is the relationship between body and soul, and how does the body figure into Carmelite spirituality? These are among the key questions to be explored in the next chapters. Now that we have taken stock of the roots of the Carmelite tradition, let us proceed.

Charism

2

The Soul, Fraternity, and Allegiance to Christ

I. THE FEMININE GENIUS OF THE SOUL

A. Discovering the Soul

AT THE HEART OF Carmelite spirituality lives the human soul.[1] As the spiritual centerpiece of the human being, the soul includes all that is unique to each individual person: personality, conscience, spiritual affectivity, intellect, memory, and will. Intimately intertwined with the body, the soul refers to all that is most interior to the self. With Teresa of Ávila's reformed Order of Discalced Carmelites came a new attentiveness to the human soul and its relationship with God. Twentieth-century French Carmelite Paul-Marie of the Cross puts it this way: "The desert of the soul is the very place of God's communication."[2] Likewise, Teresa realized that authentic Carmelite spirituality had to ponder deeply the mystery of the soul as the precise locale of communion with God. As a woman, Teresa was attuned to the interior dimensions of the person in a way that men were not. She brought these attunements to the forefront of Carmelite life, making them its trademark.

---

1. For a much more extensive treatment of the mystery of the human soul, especially in light of the philosophy and theology of the Discalced Carmelite, Saint Edith Stein, see Wallenfang, *Human and Divine Being*.

2. Paul-Marie of the Cross, *Carmelite Spirituality*, 20.

Teresa's premier work on the soul is *The Interior Castle*. She begins the work by admitting the common neglect of human beings to recognize the reality of the soul:

> It is a shame and unfortunate that through our own fault we don't understand ourselves or know who we are. Wouldn't it show great ignorance, my daughters, if someone when asked who he was didn't know, and didn't know his father or mother or from what country he came? Well now, if this would be so extremely stupid, we are incomparably more so when we do not strive to know who we are, but limit ourselves to considering only roughly these bodies. Because we have heard and because faith tells us so, we know we have souls.[3]

What was true in the sixteenth century is even more true today: the soul goes largely forgotten within the culture and among all those trinkets that it prizes most highly.[4] This becomes the first challenge for Carmelite spirituality—that we are unfamiliar with our souls and how they relate to God. Instead, we tend to be preoccupied with our physical bodies and their repertory of needs. Madison Avenue leads us to believe that with the right combination of vitamins, dietary adjustments, fitness plans, and wardrobe, we will arrive blissfully at Destination Happiness. Yet confronted with such guarantees, we are reminded of the words of Saint Paul: "Train yourself for devotion, for, while physical training is of limited value, devotion is valuable in every respect, since it holds a promise of life both for the present and for the future" (1 Tim 4:7–8).

Turning attention toward the soul is the beginning of understanding what is meant by contemplative prayer in the Carmelite tradition. Carmelites are led to ask questions such as these: What is the soul? How does the soul relate to God? What does God desire for my soul? How do I let my soul be shaped by the Holy Spirit? What are the obstacles in the way of the soul's approach to God, and how do I rid myself of these? What does it mean for a soul to be humble?

3. Teresa of Ávila, *Interior Castle*, 34.

4. See Edith Stein, *Finite and Eternal Being*, 19, 549n29. Here Stein mentions "the crisis, for example, in which psychology has found itself since the turn of the [twentieth] century is merely an inescapable consequence of the amazing feat which the psychology of the nineteenth century performed when it simply discarded the concept of the soul . . . . The attempt of psychology to divorce itself totally from all religious and theological considerations has yielded a psychology without a soul."

B. The Soul as God's Heaven

For the Carmelites, preoccupation about the soul does not mean devaluing or neglecting the importance of the body. Carmelite anthropology does not sever the integral union between soul and body.[5] Rather, by attending first to the centrality of the soul, the dignity of the body is elevated all the more.

In her celebrated prayer to God as Trinity, Elizabeth of the Trinity places the accent on the soul's relation to God: "Give peace to my soul; make it Your heaven, Your beloved dwelling and Your resting place . . . . O consuming Fire, Spirit of Love, 'come upon me,' and create in my soul a kind of incarnation of the Word: that I may be another humanity for Him in which He can renew His whole Mystery."[6] She depicts the soul itself as heaven. This is a common Carmelite conviction. Though we often consider the transcendence and distance of heaven from earth, the Carmelite paradigm inverts this tendency and regards the soul as the privileged abode of God.

Indeed, this radical paradigm shift bears great fruit for self-awareness in prayer. You begin to regard yourself as the treasure that you are—God's treasure, created to be a spiritual vessel of divine Presence, an ark of the divine Word, a womb of divine Love.

C. The Soul as Martha and Mary

In imitation of the Blessed Virgin Mary, who conceived the eternal Son of God in her virginal womb, every human soul is to become a fertile spiritual womb for the abiding and perennial gestation of divine Life. This is a difficult concept for a man to comprehend, for he has no experience of bearing a child in his own body. Man must look to woman—to the feminine genius—in order to emulate the empathic bearing of the other within the same. This signifies a universal human vocation for men and women alike: to bear the hidden Deity within the hospitable hollow of the soul.[7] Carmelite attunement to the soul awakens one to encounter the

5. See John Paul II, *Catechism,* 365: "The unity of soul and body is so profound that one has to consider the soul to be the 'form' of the body: i.e., it is because of its spiritual soul that the body made of matter becomes a living, human body; spirit and matter, in man, are not two natures united, but rather their union forms a single nature."

6. Elizabeth of the Trinity, *Complete Works,* 1:183.

7. See Nancy, *Noli me tangere,* 92: "There is a very beautiful story in religion, in what is called a mystical form of the Jewish religion known as Kabbalah. It says that god created the world not at all by making something but by withdrawing, by breathing himself

other from without and the Other from within. Teresa of Ávila never tires of referring to the complementarity between Mary, the contemplative, and Martha, the servant:

> Let us desire and be occupied in prayer not for the sake of our enjoyment but so as to have this strength to serve . . . . Believe me, Martha and Mary must join together in order to show hospitality to the Lord and to have him always present and not host him badly for failing to give him something to eat. How would Mary, always seated at his feet, provide him with food if her sister did not help her? His food is that in every way possible we draw souls that they may be saved and praise him always.[8]

Watching and waiting with great solicitude, the soul is vigilant before the other. With spiritual being as its essence, the soul is destined to take leave of itself in pursuit of the other, whether fellow human or divine Guest. The soul is at once womb and groom, mother and father, receptor and initiator of gift. Vacating its tendency toward self-indulgence and self-absorption, the soul commences its daily exodus, departing from itself through the desert of self-denial.

Paradoxically, the soul becomes its true self by leaving behind the mirage of Narcissus, inverting its suffocating paralysis of more of the same—the self and only the self. In evacuating itself from itself toward the other, one breathes life into the other (Martha) and receives the Breath of God (Mary). This is the meaning of love and responsibility as revealed by the theological architecture of Carmelite mysticism.

---

in, by emptying himself. By hollowing himself out, god opens the void in which the world can take its place. This is called the *tsim-tsum* in the Kabbalah." In a similar way, the soul must breathe itself in, hollow itself out, empty itself, if God is to be the Lord of its universe.

8. Teresa of Ávila, *Interior Castle*, 437. Cf. Teresa of Ávila, *Way of Perfection*, in *Collected Works*, 2:100–101, 155: "Saint Martha was a saint, even though they do not say she was contemplative . . . . If she had been enraptured like the Magdalene, there wouldn't have been anyone to give food to the divine Guest. Well, think of this congregation as the home of Saint Martha and that there must be people for every task . . . . Let us recall that it is necessary for someone to prepare His meal and let them consider themselves lucky to serve with Martha. Let them consider how true humility consists very much in great readiness to be content with whatever the Lord may want to do with them and in always finding oneself unworthy to be called his servant . . . . This is a great favor for those to whom the Lord grants it; the active and contemplative lives are joined. The faculties all serve the Lord together: the will is occupied in its work and contemplation without knowing how; the other two faculties [that is, the intellect and the memory] serve in the work of Martha. Thus Martha and Mary walk together."

As human beings, we are tempted toward the either-or, the one-or-the-other. Catholic theology, however, reveals a paradoxical logic of both-and. Perhaps you can have your cake and eat it, too. Saverio Cannistrà and the Definitors of the Discalced Carmelites put this notion beautifully in a 2011 letter from the definitory:

> We think of our communities subject to two forces: one centripetal which calls us to live interiorly, the other centrifugal which asks us to live for others. If both tensions are not brought into a positive equilibrium, the individual and the community can become a *sect*, the movement toward the interior prevails, or the force which called us outwards quickly *flags*. Probably, our present structure of life, founded many times on *doing* rather than *being*, as I have already written on more than one occasion, tends to lead us more towards a breakup, a de-structuring of community. As an answer, especially in younger religious, the call is felt to live more interiorly. But if this does not find a way to express itself, in a bodily manner of service, it ends up by being *sectarian* and leads to alienation and dissatisfaction in those who propose it and, in this case, express it.[9]

Appealing to the Catholic both-and of Mary and Martha, this exhortation shows the unified complementarity between the active apostolates and the irreducible vocation to contemplative prayer. Even Carmelites, who are especially contemplative at their core, are to live with the fluidity of adapting to the real needs that surround them.

A Carmelite discovers that she is called to surrender one final possession which is dearest to her as a Carmelite: her secluded life of silent prayer. This is to say that the Carmelite, out of love for God and neighbor, is perpetually open to being interrupted for a greater good. It is in these pestering interruptions that love is put to the test continually and in surprising ways. There is a delicate tug of war that takes place between the interior and the exterior, between contemplation and action, between silence and necessary speech. A faithful Carmelite is the one who is always available to the needs of other souls in love.

The Carmelite is invariably at work negotiating between these mutually inclusive needs. Just as a mother who cares for the child in her womb is at work caring for those of her children outside of her womb, so does the Carmelite simultaneously care for the infant Christ within and the

9. Cannistrà et al., *General Definitory Letter*.

languishing Christ without. To be Carmelite is to be perpetually available to the other. While anchored in the circulating presence of God, I am ever open to where the Holy Spirit might be leading me to serve. Similar to the Apostle Philip in his encounter with the Ethiopian man, the Spirit often "snatches us away" here and there to do the work of the Lord: "The wind blows where it wills, and you can hear the sound it makes, but you do not know where it comes from or where it goes; so it is with everyone who is born of the Spirit" (John 3:8).[10] This attitude of openness characterizes the spirit of the Carmelite who, though inclined to remain in contemplation like Mary, is joyfully open to being interrupted for the sake of a contemplative apostolate that cannot help but spill out of itself in loving service of the other like Martha. Saint Paul shares this sentiment as well, as he writes to the church at Philippi: "For to me life is Christ, and death is gain. If I go on living in the flesh, that means fruitful labor for me. And I do not know which I shall choose. I am caught between the two. I long to depart from this life and be with Christ, [for] that is far better. Yet that I remain [in] the flesh is more necessary for your benefit."[11] Like Teresa who says, "I die because I do not die!," Saint Paul yearns to enter into the most intimate union with Christ possible. But as long as God has other plans for him, he is fully onboard with God's will.[12] The apostolate of the Carmelite is contemplative love—a love that "is never idle," just as a mother's love for her child never ceases to grow, radiating outward and inward in a symphony of sacred togetherness.[13]

II. THE MASCULINE GENIUS OF THE SOUL

A. Meditation as Mission

If there is a feminine genius of the soul, there is also a masculine genius of the soul. While the feminine genius of interiority is informed by Teresa

10. See Acts 8:26–40, and Eccl 11:5: "Just as you do not know how the life breath enters the human frame in the mother's womb, so you do not know the work of God, who is working in everything."

11. Phil 1:21–24.

12. See Teresa of Ávila, *Poetry*, Poem 1, in *Collected Works*, 3:375–76.

13. See Teresa of Ávila, *Interior Castle*, 208: "Love is never idle, and a failure to grow would be a very bad sign. A soul that has tried to be the betrothed of God himself, that is now intimate with His Majesty, and has reached the boundaries that were mentioned, must not go to sleep."

of Ávila and the line of other female Discalced Carmelite saints, such as Thérèse of Lisieux and Teresa Benedicta of the Cross, the masculine genius of exteriority is inspired by the original band of men who founded the Carmelites and the prominent male voices which spoke ever since, in particular, that of John of the Cross. First, we must recall that the founders of Carmel were in the midst of a mission. They had gone out in faith and fortitude to rescue their brethren who were in distress and under attack in the Holy Land. Their mission then was transposed from military mandate to monastic meditation: "Each one shall remain in his cell or near it, meditating day and night on the Law of the Lord and watching in prayer, unless otherwise justly occupied."[14] Silent meditation on the law of the Lord and daily spiritual battle became their new mission (see 1 Cor 9:24–27; Eph 6:10–20).

Derived from the Latin verb *mittere*, the word mission connotes being sent forth with haste and purpose—to be launched like a missile toward a predetermined destination with great impact. Peculiar to the masculine genius, this erect dynamism of being propelled outward in mission attains to its maximum potential when oriented around serving the other in love. What a farce (Latin: *farcire*, to stuff, to fatten, to gorge oneself) it is to watch a man in mission for himself alone, for he ends up miserable and lonely, short circuiting the gift that he was meant to be for the other. A self-centered mission is no mission at all, for it never takes leave of the self, it never goes anywhere, it never gets off the ground. Instead, it stuffs itself like a gluttonous pig until it is affixed upon its own avaricious skewer. In contrast, the masculine genius, manifest above all in Christ the Bridegroom, accomplishes its mission in laying down its life for his bride (see Eph 5:25).

A Carmelite is one who has been hailed to lay down his or her life for the other in a constant and unrelenting way. Signified by the beautiful word solicitude (Latin: *sollus*, whole, entire; *ciere*, to put in motion), the Carmelite is compelled to put his whole self in motion toward the other, around the other, at the service of the other, for the sake of the other, for the good of the other. Just as "the Son of Man did not come to be served but to serve and to give his life as a ransom for many" (Mark 10:45), the Carmelite gives up so many of life's self-serving pleasures in order to become a pure gift of himself for the other, desiring to substitute himself for the other to save the other. This happens every day through vicarious—representative—prayer

14. Albert of Jerusalem, *Carmelite Rule*, ¶ 5.

and sacrifice on behalf of the other. As a Carmelite, I always stand in the stead of the other before God, for I am "my brother's keeper" (Gen 4:9).

B. Fraternity

Among the defining traits of the Carmelite charism are fraternity and allegiance to Christ. Fraternity refers to familial bonds formed among those who live united in the communal contemplative life. The original Carmelites were established as a brotherhood and vowed their lives to God and to one another. It is a love that is celestially familial and transcends even that of family ties. Rooted in the initiatory power of baptism, Carmelite fraternity places one in intimate contact with the host of angels and saints that comprise the mystical Body of Christ. It is a family within a family, a communion within a communion.

Just as there are distinct orders of angelic beings—for example, seraphim, cherubim, thrones, dominions, etc.—there are also distinct orders of human beings within the church, based on the difference and complementarity of charisms that constitute the sacred hierarchy, including clergy and laity, of the church.[15] The Carmelites embody the heart of the contemplative order of Christian discipleship, performing the work of prayer to the most intensified degrees. They are the quiet center of the church which sustains and inspires the active aspects of the body, such as pastoral outreach and all of the mendicant apostolates.

For Carmelites, contemplative prayer is the primary apostolate, but it is always prayer for the sake of the diversified and suffering body of Christ. Paul-Marie of the Cross puts it this way: "Carmelite spirituality is not contemplative *and* apostolic. It is apostolic *because* it is contemplative."[16] The Carmelite apostolate is contemplation in itself, but a kind of contemplation that spills out of solitude and seclusion because of ardent love for the other. How often in the Gospels do we observe Jesus withdrawing from the crowds to pray, only to return to the crowds in great love? Fellowship fosters contemplative prayer, and contemplative prayer fuels the fruitfulness of fellowship. It is the fraternal character of the Carmelite Order that holds it together as a unified community of contemplatives.

15. See Pseudo-Dionysius, *Celestial Hierarchy,* in *Complete Works,* 143–92; and *Ecclesiastical Hierarchy,* in *Complete Works,* 193–260.

16. Paul-Marie of the Cross, *Carmelite Spirituality,* 81.

C. Allegiance to Christ

Along with fraternity, allegiance to Christ is a common term used in reference to the Carmelite charism. It describes the zealous and passionate disposition of the Carmelite, akin to the zeal of Elijah that defended the resolute faith in the one, true, and living God on Mount Carmel (see 1 Kgs 18–19). It is not only a zeal which defends and protects, but one that loves with divine intensity. As the religious suffix OCD playfully suggests, Discalced Carmelites are "obsessive-compulsive" about God and the things of God. They are so obsessive-compulsive that their love for God keeps them up at night, makes them forget to eat, and makes them desire to suffer for the sake of the world. It is an uncanny and unnatural disposition that is forgetful of self and disenchanted with the things of this world. Like Christ, the Carmelites claim to have a most nourishing food that goes largely unknown: "My food is to do the will of the one who sent me and to finish his work" (John 4:34). Carmelites are called to forsake all else in single-minded and wholehearted devotion to God. All faculties of body and soul are to be dedicated to the will of God. It is a vocation to die with Christ so that all who accept the summons may be risen freely with Christ (see Rom 6:8; Gal 2:19–20). Carmelites are bound and obligated to Christ as their lone King. Sharing a common genus with Ignatian spirituality, the military motif informs the meaning of allegiance to Christ and to his mission.

According to the gestalt of its masculine genius, Carmelites are like the Navy SEALs and the Marines of the church as she remains within the fray of spiritual combat. Carmelites are on the front lines of spiritual warfare. They "pommel (their) bod(ies) and subdue (them)" so that they stay within the will of God and act as collaborators with Christ in the redemption of the world (1 Cor 9:24–27). Secular Discalced Carmelites go about this battle with great flexibility and versatility. We are ever pliable before God, yielding to the marching orders of the day, even when they often tug at the serenity of our desire for long periods of solitude and undisturbed prayer. OCDS members are used to adaptation, responding to many needs and duties within the secular realm, all the while sanctifying it. Through our contemplative gaze of the world, we hallow the world by living in it. We take that which has been rendered profane and breathe life into it by loving it. We are appointed as daily martyrs of love, and we rest in our work of love. Distracted by nothing and attracted to everything, we give our flesh as food for the other. No matter our state of life, we are always mother and father to the other, welcoming him, feeding him, being for him. What a strange paradox, this nearness through remoteness and desertion, wherein the other is rescued from abandonment by abandoning him. This is to say that by denying the divinity of everything that is not divine, we divinize it. By renouncing the idol of creation, it is made icon through which to approach the divine.

This, too, is paradox: that we defeat our enemies not by destroying them but by loving them. What is defeated is not the otherness of the other but the reduction of the other to the same. By loving the other, I am saying that the other is not me and cannot be reduced to me. If I have an enemy, it is because I am wanting to reduce him to me, or he is wanting to reduce me to him, or both. Love renounces the temptation of reducing all to the same. Through Christ and the Holy Spirit, God is revealed as an eternal union of diverse Persons—a diversity which cannot be reduced to unity and a unity which is accomplished precisely in and through diversity. The same plus the same does not equal unity, but only more of the same. Things must be different in order to bring about a genuine bonded unity. The Carmelite recognizes this as the logic of the entire cosmos—the logic of love—and exercises this logic through his or her daily life. Love approaches God, the Other within, and the neighbor, the other without. Interiority and exteriority join together as the twofold movement of love—a movement at once united and differentiated, the feminine and the masculine genius of the soul.

D. Saint Joseph

Intimately related to the masculine genius of the soul is Saint Joseph, the chaste earthly father of Jesus and protector of the Holy Family. Next to the Blessed Virgin Mary, Saint Joseph holds pride of place among the Carmelite devotions. Teresa of Jesus named her first Discalced monastery in Ávila after Saint Joseph in 1562. Reference to Saint Joseph figures significantly within Teresa's writings. For instance, in her autobiography she writes,

> Because of my impressive experience of the goods this glorious saint obtains from God, I had the desire to persuade all to be devoted to him . . . . Especially persons of prayer should always be attached to him. For I don't know how one can think about the Queen of Angels and about when she went through so much with the Infant Jesus without giving thanks to Saint Joseph for the good assistance he then provided them both with. Those who cannot

find a master to teach them prayer should take this glorious saint for their master, and they will not go astray.[17]

How is it that Teresa could recommend such devotion to a saint so hidden from our view historically? None of his words come down to us through the biblical witness. Only four scenes are offered to imagination, three from the Gospel of Matthew and one from the Gospel of Luke: Joseph's dreams and obedience to lead the Holy Family out of harm's way (see Matt 1:18–25; 2:13–15, 19–23; Luke 2:41–52).

However, at least four striking points are made in these texts. First, Joseph is described as "a righteous man." Given the context, Joseph is considered to be a faithful observer of Mosaic law, the Torah, and he is attentive to God's will in all things. Second, he overcomes his doubt and fear over Mary's pregnancy. Knowing the child has not been conceived from his seed, he trusts her testimony nevertheless and believes the child to be of supernatural origin. Moreover, he assumes responsibility for Mary's well-being by not wanting to expose her to shame. Third, Joseph is depicted as obedient to the command of God given him through his dreams. In Luke's narrative, Joseph utters no words but simply does as the angel of the Lord commanded him. Like Joseph, the masculine genius is attentive, obedient, and responsive to the mission assigned. Fourth, Joseph is said to have named the child upon his birth. In naming him Jesus, Joseph claims him as his own, even by way of adoption, and pronounces the meaning of this infant for the world: Jesus, YHWH-saves.

Elsewhere in Scripture, we learn that Joseph was a carpenter (see Matt 13:55) and that he taught Jesus this craft, since Jesus is called a carpenter as well. We infer that Joseph must have died before Jesus's passion and death because he is not at the foot of the cross alongside Mary, where he certainly would have been if he had remained alive. Altogether, the visage of Joseph is mysterious—always behind the scenes but no doubt very prominent in the lives of Jesus and Mary. He is faithful to them and he husbands the Holy Family and, therefore, the church. Like the Carmelites, Joseph is hidden from view. He is quiet and humble. Rather than speak much, he simply does what he is instructed by God. We can imagine Joseph always in quiet contemplation, whether while at work or at rest. As man of the house, he bears the weight of responsibility for all inside. He is their protector, servant, and guide. He is the strong support of a father for which every human family yearns. Like Elijah, John the Baptist, and his bride Mary, Joseph is

17. Teresa of Ávila, *Life*, in *Collected Works,* 1:80–81.

Carmelite through and through. He is the epitome of proximity to Jesus and Mary, vigilant in his post to pour out his life as gift for them.

The masculine genius of the soul acts always *in persona Ioseph*—Joseph the advocate, Joseph the caretaker of other, Joseph the warrior in prayer, Joseph the righteous one, Joseph as responsible for all. In his quiet and hidden life, Joseph is hard at work, never tiring of the mission set before him to love and to protect those in his charge. And so it is for the Carmelite: ever vigilant, ever on guard against the wickedness and snares of the enemy, ever watchful for the next directive to serve. Like Joseph, the faithful Carmelite remembers God "through the watches of the night" (Ps 63:7).

3

Humility, Responsibility, and the Cross

I. HUMILITY AND THE THEOLOGY OF CHILDHOOD

> My son, conduct your affairs with humility, and you will be loved
> more than a giver of gifts. Humble yourself the more, the greater
> you are, and you will find mercy in the sight of God. Many are lofty
> and famous, but to the humble he reveals his plan. For great is the
> power of the Lord; by the humble he is glorified.
> Sir 3:17–20

NEXT TO LOVE IN the order of virtues, the second in rank for the Carmelite daily walk is humility. Humility would have it no other way. Based on its Latin root (*humus*—earth, dirt, clay, ground, soil), the word humility signifies groundedness and lowliness. It means at once stability and fragility. The word human is derived from the same Latin root. To be human is to be fashioned from the dust of the ground: "Then the LORD God formed the man out of the dust of the ground and blew into his nostrils the breath of life, and the man became a living being. . . . For you are dust, and to dust you shall return" (Gen 2:7; 3:19). As human beings, we are both the most powerful creatures on earth and the most vulnerable. Our paradoxical nature, created in the image of God, mirrors the paradoxical shape of divine revelation: God, who shows his incomprehensible power and majesty through the frail flesh of human nature, body and soul. By his incarnation, the eternal Word of the Father became flesh to accomplish the most magnificent manifestation of the divine nature within the order of

27

creation. Two natures united irrevocably by the uncreated personhood of the pre-existent Son of the Father proclaims one of the greatest mysteries about God: humility describes his raiment and heart. "Take my yoke upon you and learn from me, for I am meek and humble of heart; and you will find rest for yourselves" (Matt 11:29). Humility is the code that grants access to the peaceful rest of God: "God resists the proud, but gives grace to the humble" (James 4:6; 1 Pet 5:5).

Because it is self-forgetful, humility is other-aware. A humble man seeks not to bring glory to himself but to God alone. Humility cultivates reverence of speech, custody of the eyes, and self-mastery of the heart. Humility is neither boastful nor arrogant, neither greedy nor gross, neither self-insulating nor self-absorbed. Humility is enveloped in hiddenness: "It is the glory of God to conceal a matter, and the glory of kings to fathom a matter" (Prov 25:2). Carmelites are content with hiddenness because humility flourishes in "a garden enclosed, a fountain sealed" (Song 4:12). Carmel—the garden of God—is content to be just that: a secret, quiet garden giving praise to its divine soil (Father), light (Son), and water (Holy Spirit). The tiny flower brings glory to her creator whether or not she is seen by unsuspecting passersby. Both reflecting and absorbing the light of the sun, the little flower exalts her uncaused Cause, without which she is not. Humility remembers that "man is but a breath, his days are like a passing shadow" (Ps 144:4), and that "the grass withers, the flower wilts, but the word of our God stands forever" (Isa 40:8). Yet humility's paradox is that it remains anchored in the storm.

While ever reckoning with the fact that life is transient and ephemeral, humility abides in confidence and courage: "Yet the world and its enticement are passing away. But whoever does the will of God remains forever" (1 John 2:17). Like the unleavened bread of Passover become Eucharist, humility is not puffed up by inflated hubris or coarse humor. Instead, humility reminds a person "not to think of himself more highly than one ought to think, but to think soberly, each according to the measure of faith God has apportioned" (Rom 12:3). A humble man counts his words because he knows that each word counts. A humble man keeps his eyes on his own work because he knows that "the word of God is now at work in him who believes" (1 Thess 2:13). A humble man holds his tongue because he knows that a "tongue of fire" is holding him (see Acts 2:3). "Trust in the LORD with all your heart, on your own intelligence do not rely; in all your ways be mindful of him, and he will make straight your paths" (Prov 3:5–6).

Humility trusts in the Lord because it knows that the Lord has entrusted us with his promises that never fail. Humility is a child who trusts in the goodness of her father and mother, for the child knows that this is her very vocation without even knowing the meaning of the word vocation.

Humility, as a child, avoids both the errors of neo-Gnosticism and neo-Pelagianism.[1] In contrast to the former, humility resists spiritual worldliness and religious elitism. Like Saint Paul, a humble man works out his salvation "with fear and trembling" (Phil 2:12). Salvation is not reduced to a set of formulas, a doctrinal index, or a fundamentalist grammar that listens only with its own mouth. The humble man does not cast judgment on the world and all the while exonerate and excuse himself. The humble man does not reduce truth to an ideology to which he alone holds the passcode, lock and key. "Blind guides, who strain out the gnat and swallow the camel!" (Matt 23:24). In contrast to the latter, that is, in contrast to neo-Pelagianism, humility gives credit where credit is due: always to the grace of God and never to the self. As Jesus says to us in the Gospel of Saint John: "I am the vine, you are the branches. Whoever remains in me and I in him will bear much fruit, because without me you can do nothing" (John 15:5). In this case, though "faith without works is dead" (James 2:26), faith reduced to works is also dead and futile. "All our just deeds are like polluted rags" (Isa 64:5). And the Lord speaks to us: "When you have done all you have been commanded, say, 'We are unprofitable servants; we have done what we were obliged to do'" (Luke 17:10). At the same time, as a child, humility binds itself to truth that is never sunk beneath the shifting seas of relativism. Humility serves as the gateway to the truth inasmuch as it resists the tempting facile reductionism of the whole to only one or some of its many parts and as it insists on letting all of the diverse parts be reunited according to their common whole.

"Amen, I say to you, unless you turn and become like children, you will not enter the kingdom of heaven" (Matt 18:3). Humility fosters a theology of childhood because "whoever humbles himself like a child is the greatest in the kingdom of heaven" (Matt 18:4). A child, in herself, because she constantly testifies to divine providence in her desperate neediness and majestic smallness, serves as the model Carmelite contemplative. Within her mystical cloister of the world, the child embraces the All, for all lights up according to the radical and active passivity of the gaze, taste, touch,

---

1. See Congregation for Doctrine of Faith, *Placuit Deo*; Francis, *Gaudete et exsultate*, 36–62; Francis, *Evangelii gaudium*, 93–97, 233.

smell, and audiophility of the child. For the child, the world is a playground since, recalling the beginning of creation, divine Wisdom testifies: "When (God) fixed the foundations of earth, then was I beside him as artisan; I was his delight day by day, playing before him all the while, playing over the whole of his earth, having my delight with human beings. Now, children, listen to me; happy are they who keep my ways" (Prov 8:29–32). We are adopted children of God insofar as we are children of Wisdom, and, like Wisdom, we are reinvigorated by our primordial vocation to play throughout this spacious universe of creation as within a womb of living delights, "for the praise of the glory of his grace that he granted us in the beloved" (Eph 1:6). Like Saint Elizabeth of the Trinity, we are ennobled to become "praises of glory" before "the crucified Lord of glory" (1 Cor 2:2, 8).

The theology of childhood, or *Kindertheologie*, is innate for the child, but the adult must live into it, all the while growing older in years. *Kindertheologie* is characterized by the primacy of religious manifestation and the predilection for silence. It is not in a hurry but instead savors every moment. It delights in the smallest tokens of affection and the most hidden baubles of beauty. It is pure passivity before a world that gives itself as a medley of prizes to the contemplative soul. *Kindertheologie* describes the life of the child that abides daily and nightly in communion with the Most Holy Trinity even without being able to articulate the prosaic doctrine thereof. That Saint John the Apostle does not tire in referring to the faithful as "children of God" underscores even more the fact that redemption is a movement toward the theological genius of the child.[2] In its most tender and secret stage, *Kindertheologie* is revealed in the life of the infant in her mother's womb and during the weeks directly following birth. Over the days just after birth, nourished by the nutrient-rich colostrum flowing from her mother's breasts, the infant points us to what is most essential, the *unum necessarium* of the spiritual life. And what is the one thing necessary? Docile receptivity to gift. Being entrusted with the richest and purest of all the gifts. *Kindertheologie* reawakens us to our own *Oberweis* Lost.[3]

---

2. See, for instance, 1 John 3:1–3: "See what love the Father has bestowed on us that we may be called the children of God. Yet so we are. The reason the world does not know us is that it did not know him. Beloved, we are God's children now; what we shall be has not yet been revealed. We do know that when it is revealed we shall be like him, for we shall see him as he is. Everyone who has this hope based on him makes himself pure, as he is pure."

3. The phrase "*Oberweis* Lost" is a play on the title of John Milton's epic poem *Paradise Lost*. The German name *Oberweis*, derived from *ober* (upper/higher) and *weisen*

It is fitting to reference two of Karl Rahner's essays that are quite relevant to the topic at hand: "Ideas for a Theology of Childhood" and "Christmas, the Festival of Eternal Youth." In the former essay, Rahner insists that childhood is not a time of life to outgrow or to let fade into a forgotten past. Instead, he writes that "we do not lose childhood as that which recedes ever further into our past, that which remains behind as we advance forward in time, but rather we go towards it as that which has been achieved in time and redeemed forever in time. We only *become* the children whom we *were* because we gather up in time—and in this our childhood too—into our eternity."[4] Rahner's claim about the dual maturation toward both adulthood and childhood resonates with the Hebrew notion of eternity—עוֹלָם (*olam*)—that connotes at once futurity and antiquity. This is the paradoxical nature of time as revealed in the Jewish theological tradition. It is multidirectional, multidimensional. Liturgical tempo encompasses all time in such a comprehensive way that to move in one direction is to move in all directions.[5] The season of childhood is indispensable for the liturgical actor. Childhood is destined to be reinvigorated at every moment to ensure immunity from the sway of the natural attitude.

In the tenor of the child, Rahner perceives the history of one's personal childhood to form the bedrock of all ensuing life-experience: Childhood "is important in itself also, as a stage of man's personal history in which that takes place which can only take place in childhood itself, a field which bears fair flowers and ripe fruits such as can only grow in *this* field and in no other, and which will themselves be carried into the storehouses of eternity .... *This* morning does not derive its life simply from the afternoon which follows."[6] The sui generis character of childhood preserves its dawn of meaning throughout the course of life—a course anchored in the eternal morning of redemption, the greatest possibility. To begin to experience this twilight of redemption in the here and now demands infinite openness to possibility—above all, openness to the possibility of forgiveness, reconciliation, healing, and transfiguration: "Childhood is openness. Human childhood is infinite openness. The mature childhood of the adult is the

---

(to show), *wissen* (to know), *weiß* (white), or *Wesen* (being) can mean "to show/know above or beyond," "to show/know beyond being," "the highest mode of being or the most actualized form of being," and "the whitest/purest (milk)."

4. Rahner, "Ideas for a Theology of Childhood" in *Further Theology* 2, 36.

5. See Wallenfang, *Dialectical Anatomy*, 173–76.

6. Rahner, *Further Theology* 2, 36.

attitude in which we bravely and trustfully maintain an infinite openness in all circumstances and despite the experiences of life which seem to invite us to close ourselves."[7] This radical openness of which Rahner speaks is an appeal to the Carmelite phenomenological attitude that overcomes, by way of daily conversion, the concupiscent force of the natural attitude. And for Christian theology, this victory is won by a child-king who ushers in the reign of the possible once and for all: The Christ "child is one in whom the eternal youth of God breaks in upon this world definitively and victoriously; into this world, which seems only able to go on living in that the death of one of its inhabitants makes way for another to be born."[8] Grace is the word used to describe this unmatchable process wherein the eternal youth of God comingles with one's own. Death is overcome by its own death, resulting in eternal life, just as impossibility is rendered impossible by possibility's power to cancel cancelation. In the manifestation of the eternal life of God in the Christ-child, death is revealed as a temporary interruption to the perpetual flow of life from eternity. Phenomenological givenness—accessible to the degree of contemplative perception—attests to this eternal life as gift and is recognized most of all by the uninhibited life of the child. As masterful contemplative, the child invites us to reenter the dialectical dance of mystical interpretation where "the one who is least (μικρότερος) among all of you is the one who is the greatest (μέγας)."[9] Yet it is the scandal of the cross that links this theology of childhood to its complementary counterpart, the theology of adulthood, to which we will now turn.

II. RESPONSIBILITY AND THE THEOLOGY OF ADULTHOOD

> Then the LORD asked Cain, "Where is your brother Abel?" He answered, "I do not know. Am I my brother's keeper?"
> Gen 4:9

---

7. Rahner, *Further Theology 2*, 48. Cf. 50: "In the child a man begins who must undergo the wonderful adventure of remaining a child forever, becoming a child to an ever-increasing extent, making his childhood of God real and effective in this childhood of his, for this is the task of his maturity."

8. Rahner, "Christmas, the Festival of Eternal Youth" in *Further Theology 1*, 121. See Luke 1:37: "For nothing will be impossible (οὐκ ἀδυνατήσει) for God."

9. Luke 9:48.

As a corollary and complement to a theology of childhood that flows from the virtue of humility, a theology of adulthood completes the face of Christian discipleship. Just as a spiritual maturity obtains in the child, a complementary ripeness is meant to develop into adulthood over the course of created time, without leaving behind but continuing to grow into the spiritual maturity of childhood. Saint Paul writes, "Brothers, I could not talk to you as spiritual people, but as fleshly people, as infants in Christ. I fed you milk, not solid food, because you were unable to take it," (1 Cor 3:1–2), and, again, "When I was a child, I used to talk as a child, think as a child, reason as a child; when I became a man, I put aside childish things," (1 Cor 13:11). The author to the Hebrews says similar things: "Although you should be teachers by this time, you need to have someone teach you again the basic elements of the utterances of God. You need milk, and not solid food. Everyone who lives on milk lacks the experience of the word of righteousness, for he is a child. But solid food is for the mature, for those whose faculties are trained by practice to discern good and evil" (Heb 5:12–14). In all these biblical instances, a theology of adulthood is put forward that implies a maturation of discipleship and steadfast fidelity to Jesus and his Mother according to the full stature of spiritual development. Without scorning the spiritual profundity of the child (even if such biblical passages have been misinterpreted historically as doing so), the biblical authors seek to call our attention to the peculiarity of spiritual mastery in the key of adulthood. It is a shame that the adjective adult, as in adult books and adult videos, has taken on a connotation of the pornographic and a perverted anthropology. As if one needs to have become an adult to handle the levels of violence, depravity, and abjection presented in such materials. Rather, authentic adulthood is precisely the personal responsibility that renounces such evils for the sake of faithfully stewarding the wholeness and integrity of the Good. Adults are those charged generationally with safeguarding the child. To become an adult is to have become responsible and accountable for the child—to have become answerable for the world. It is to have become a father or a mother in relation to the vulnerable other.

The theology of adulthood, or *Altertheologie*, without disdaining the theology of childhood, values ethical maturity above the contemplative proclivity of the child. In contrast to the passive disposition of *Kindertheologie*, *Altertheologie* is intentional and active. *Altertheologie* is rooted in aged responsibility for the other who faces me. It is characterized by kerygmatic proclamation and the desacralization of the idolatrous tendencies of affectivity. It moves according to rigorous reason rather than intoxicating emotion. It fixates on speech, word, text, and testimony. Instead of counting its words, it multiplies them. It tends toward Scripture even more than sacrament. *Altertheologie* is fatherhood and motherhood in relation to childhood. It signifies the full flowering of virtue in the form of deliberate self-donating personal being come of age. Its facial furrows attest to the trowel of responsibility exercised across the dilation of time. *Altertheologie* blossoms from its Jewish roots of Torah that are enacted through the bar mitzvah and bat mitzvah rites of passage into religious adulthood. With this rite of passage, I take ownership of all of my moral actions. I become a man of the law. I bind my flesh to the teachings of YHWH handed on to me by my ancestors, symbolized by wrapping my body with the *tefillin* of the sacred text. *Altertheologie* is a complement to *Kindertheologie*. Without fatherhood and motherhood, there would be no childhood; without childhood, there would be no fatherhood and motherhood. Without *Altertheologie*, no *Kindertheologie*; without *Kindertheologie*, no *Altertheologie*.[10]

This dialectical complementarity between a theology of childhood and a theology of adulthood takes on a particular cast in Carmelite spirituality. While the Carmelite is called to the original innocence, naïveté, and radical passivity of the child (even the infant), at the same time, the Carmelite is summoned to the active, sober, and stern demands of adult responsibility for the other. This is the bilateral maturity of the Carmelite soul. Jesus indicates this twofold movement of the Christ-life when he says, "Behold, I send you out as sheep in the midst of wolves; so be wise as serpents and innocent as doves" (Matt 10:16). Responsibility for the other defines the universal Christian vocation of the man and the woman come of age. The Carmelite way is comprised of equally heightened degrees of silent contemplation and sonorous sociality and service of the neighbor. Though the Discalced Carmelite apostolate is essentially contemplation itself, it is a contemplation in which "we break down walls and our heart is filled with faces and names!" and that "sets out anew, to pass beyond what

10. For more discussion on the distinction between the theology of childhood and the theology of adulthood, especially in phenomenological terms of manifestation and proclamation, involving analysis of the work of Jean-Luc Marion, Paul Ricoeur, and Emmanuel Levinas, see Wallenfang, *Dialectical Anatomy of the Eucharist*; Wallenfang, *Phenomenology*; Wallenfang, *Emmanuel*; Wallenfang, *Trilectic of Testimony*; Wallenfang, "Levinas and Marion on Law and Freedom"; Wallenfang, "Face Off for Interreligious Dialogue"; and Wallenfang, "Figures and Forms of Ultimacy."

is familiar, to the fringes and beyond."[11] French Discalced Carmelite Paul-Marie of the Cross, with reference to the *Carmelite Rule of Saint Albert of Jerusalem*, recalls that "the only reason Carmelites are allowed to interrupt their 'meditation on the Law of the Lord,' and leave for a time the silence and recollected solitude of their cells, is for the salvation of souls" and that "apostolic zeal and love for souls is the proof *par excellence* that the divine presence has kindled the heart."[12]

Carmelite contemplation is other-centered—always directed to the otherness of God and the otherness of the human face that faces the monastic contemplative. This is a Carmelite paradox evidenced in the life of Jesus: "When Jesus heard of (the death of John the Baptist), he withdrew in a boat to a deserted place by himself. The crowds heard of this and followed him on foot from their towns. When he disembarked and saw the vast crowd, his heart was moved with pity for them, and he cured their sick" (Matt 14:13–14). In the Gospel accounts, Jesus often is found withdrawing to places of solitude to commune with God the Father and God the Holy Spirit through his own divinity and incarnate humanity as God the Son. Yet this solitary setting is not in opposition to the needs of people, but it is the very foundation of healing and restoration. When Jesus withdraws into solitude, it is only to welcome the crowd of his beloved sheep all the more: "Come away by yourselves to a deserted place and rest a while. . . . When Jesus disembarked and saw the vast crowd, his heart was moved with pity for them, for they were like sheep without a shepherd; and he began to teach them many things" (Mark 6:31, 34). So much contemplation, so much healing and evangelization. So much solitude, so much sociality. So much silence, so much sound.

In 1938, four years prior to her own martyrdom, in reference to the Holocaust of her own Jewish people, Saint Teresa Benedicta of the Cross wrote to Ursuline Sister Mother Petra Brüning, "I thought that those who recognized it as the cross of Christ had to take it upon themselves in the name of all."[13] Another way to say this is: "Those who are familiar with the cross of Christ should take it up on behalf of those who know nothing about it." Here Saint Teresa Benedicta of the Cross echoes a sentiment

---

11. Francis, *Evangelii gaudium*, 274, and *Gaudete et exsultate*, 135.

12. Paul-Marie of the Cross, *Carmelite Spirituality*, 32, 80. Cf. Albert of Jerusalem, *Carmelite Rule*: "Each one shall remain in his cell or near it, meditating day and night on the Law of the Lord and watching in prayer, unless otherwise justly occupied."

13. Stein, *Self-Portrait in Letters (1916–1942)*, 295.

similar to that of Saint Paul: "Now I rejoice in my sufferings for your sake, and in my flesh I am filling up what is lacking in the afflictions of Christ on behalf of his body, which is the church" (Col 1:24), and elsewhere, "For I could wish that I myself were accursed and separated from Christ for the sake of my brothers, my kin according to the flesh" (Rom 9:3). This is what Christian theology calls vicarious atonement—suffering on behalf of another person for the sake of his or her redemption. This is also what is meant by compassion (Latin: *com-pati*, to bear, be patient, or suffer with)— to suffer with another person in complete empathy, solidarity, intimacy, forbearance, and steadfastness. This, too, is the Carmelite vocation: to pray as one of the weeping women alongside the Blessed Virgin Mary and Saint John the Apostle at the foot of the cross of Christ on Mount Golgotha. The Carmelite is reacquainted perpetually with the cross of Christ on behalf of people who are ignorant and unfamiliar with this *axis mundi* of creation redeemed. The Carmelite vocation is "to stand proxy for sinners through voluntary and joyous suffering, and to cooperate in the salvation of humankind," and to substitute oneself for the other for the sake of the other's ongoing conversion and salvation.[14] The Carmelite substitutes himself or herself on behalf of those who have yet to encounter the fullness of divine revelation and their divinely appointed destiny. "But God proves his love for us in that while we were still sinners Christ died for us" (Rom 5:8). God did not wait until we became morally perfect to die for us, but rather, his atoning death itself empowers us toward moral perfection. So does the Carmelite adopt the cruciform posture of heart, pleading before the throne of grace, alongside Our Lady of Mount Carmel, for renewed outpourings of divine mercy upon all forlorn flesh (see Heb 4:16). The Litany of Our Lady of Mount Carmel says as much:

> Our Lady of Mount Carmel, advocate of the most abandoned sinners, pray for us sinners.
> For the hardened in vice, with confidence we come to thee, O Lady of Mount Carmel.
> For those who offend thy divine Son, with confidence we come to thee, O Lady of Mount Carmel.
> For those who neglect to pray, with confidence we come to thee, O Lady of Mount Carmel.
> For those who are in agony, with confidence we come to thee, O Lady of Mount Carmel.

14. Stein, *Self-Portrait in Letters (1916–1942)*, 128.

For those who defer their conversion, with confidence we come to
thee, O Lady of Mount Carmel.
For those suffering in purgatory, with confidence we come to thee,
O Lady of Mount Carmel.
For those who do not know thee, with confidence we come to thee,
O Lady of Mount Carmel.

The Discalced Carmelite walks with feet unshod to signify a heart
unshod in loving abandonment for the abandoned. The desperate cry of
the other person who faces me does not cease its piercing punctuation on
this side of eternity, just as there is no cessation of the steeple bell's clarion
call to prayer that punctuates the day and the night. A Carmelite awakes in
the morning in prayer and retires for the night in prayer. The psalmist puts
it well:

In the silent hours of the night, bless the Lord.
O come, bless the Lord, all you who serve the Lord,
who stand in the house of the Lord, in the courts of the house of our God.
Lift up your hands to the holy place and bless the Lord through the night.
May the Lord bless you from Zion, he who made both heaven and earth.[15]

Rooted in Judaism and in the exigencies of the Torah, responsibility
for the other is reinforced and revealed to the greatest measure in Jesus
Christ, who "had to become like his brothers in every way, that he might
be a merciful and faithful high priest before God to expiate the sins of
the people. Because he himself was tested through what he suffered, he is
able to help those who are being tested" (Heb 2:17–18).[16] The Carmelite,
in imitatio Christi, gazes upon the Crucified, listens with obedience to the
Crucified, and lets himself or herself be crucified in unification with the
Crucified for the sake of the crucified and crucifiers of the world.

15. See Ps 134 and Paul VI, *Liturgy of the Hours*, "After Evening Prayer I on Sundays."
16. Cf. Heb 2:10, 4:14–16: "For it was fitting that he, for whom and through whom all
things exist, in bringing many children to glory, should make the leader to their salvation
perfect through suffering.... Therefore, since we have a great high priest who has passed
through the heavens, Jesus, the Son of God, let us hold fast to our confession. For we do
not have a high priest who is unable to sympathize with our weaknesses, but one who
has similarly been tested in every way, yet without sin. So let us confidently approach the
throne of grace to receive mercy and to find grace for timely help."

III. BEHOLD THE BEAUTIFUL CROSS OF WOOD

> But I will bring Israel back to its pasture, to feed on Carmel and Bashan,
> and on Mount Ephraim and Gilead, until they have their fill.
> Jer 50:19

> Shepherd your people with your staff, the flock of your heritage,
> that lives apart in a woodland, in the midst of Carmel. Let them
> feed in Bashan and Gilead, as in the days of old.
> Mic 7:14

Why is the suffering and death of Jesus, the eternal Son of God become man, so tragic? It is because he is the Lord of life through whom all good things come. So, to understand the meaning of the cross, in all of its multifaceted dimensions, we must begin and end with goodness, enjoyment, and happiness. From the years of childhood onward, we are trained in the gift of enjoyment: first, the natural enjoyment of natural goods; second, the supernatural enjoyment of supernatural goods; and third, the ultimate and absolute enjoyment of our ultimate and absolute Good, namely, God. And this is the paradox of the cross: the death of death restores life. As the symbol of absolute tragedy and of complete redemption, the cross is the gateway to all beatitude. And this is the beauty of the cross: as the most concentrated, consummated, perfected, and exquisite expression of love, the cross is at once the absorption of all tragedy and the fountainhead of all triumph. Because it is the centerpiece of the created universe and of history redeemed, the cross is the delight of delights and the instigator of all joy. By lying prostrate at the foot of the cross, all fears and anxieties are quelled: "Cast all your cares upon him because he cares for you" (1 Pet 5:7). *Sans souci*—without worry, trouble, anxiety, or disquietude. By the invincible remedy of the cross, all restless worries and dreadful terrors are quieted and stilled. Through the cross, what would stifle the soul is itself stifled. Through the cross, we remain serene in the fray. The cross is the veritable tree of life.[17] At the heart of paradise is the tree of life, and it is from this tree that we are meant to eat: "I came so that they might have life and have it more abundantly" (John 10:10). Because the cross signifies the cancellation of trauma and tragedy, precisely through divine empathy and solidarity with trauma and tragedy, it is the bountiful table upon which the feast of all concupiscentless enjoyment is spread. Enjoyment of the elemental.

17. See Gen 2:8–9; 3:22–24; Prov 3:13–18; 11:30; 13:12; 15:4; Rev 2:7; 22:1–2, 14–19.

Enjoyment of friendship, fraternity, and interpersonal communion. Enjoyment of all ordered goods as gifts from God. Enjoyment of the Most Holy Trinity above all else. True enjoyment is accompanied by thanksgiving to "God, who richly provides us with all things for our enjoyment" (1 Tim 6:17). In effect, the suffering of suffering is enjoyment. Yet this is a kind of enjoyment that surpasses what is typically understood by the word enjoyment. What we are talking about is "something safer and more precious on this earth than enjoyment (see Matthew 20:22)."[18] It is a passion beyond passion. By the logic of the double negative, the passion of the cross restores all the enjoyments of paradise lost—the completest of which is the personal and communal enjoyment of the Most Holy Trinity.[19]

It is not that the cross precipitates a glossing over tragedy. Rather, the cross, first of all, welcomes a pondering over tragedy in all of its incomprehension, loss, and emotional torment and turbulence. It is necessary to participate in "sitting *shiva*" with the one who suffers, even if that one happens to be yourself, just as Job's three friends sat low with him for seven days of mourning over all of his losses.[20] We have much to learn from each episode of suffering, especially those episodes that do not come and go, but last for a lifetime. Suffering escorts and accompanies us to the threshold of the beatific mountain called heaven:

> On this mountain the LORD of hosts will provide for all peoples a feast of rich food and choice wines, juicy, rich food and pure, choice wines. On this mountain he will destroy the veil that veils all peoples, the web that is woven over all nations. He will destroy death forever. The LORD God will wipe away the tears from all faces; the reproach of his people he will remove from the whole earth; for the LORD has spoken. On that day it will be said: "Indeed, this is our God; we looked to him, and he saved us! This is the LORD to whom we looked; let us rejoice and be glad that he has saved us!" (Isa 25:6–9)[21]

The promise of this passage from Isaiah is that we will not go hungry and thirsty in the kingdom to come; we will not politicize one another by ideological strongholds in the kingdom to come; we will not die anymore

---

18. John of the Cross, *Ascent of Mount Carmel*, in *Collected Works*, II.7.6, 171.

19. For more on the notion of "the logic of the double negative," see Wallenfang, *Human and Divine Being*, 26–53, and Wallenfang, *Phenomenology*, 73–99.

20. See Job 2:11–13.

21. Cf. Rev 21:1–27.

in the kingdom to come; we will not be filled with sorrow and mourning in the kingdom to come; we will not be beset by mental illnesses and neuroses in the kingdom to come; but we will rejoice heartily there! This promise of God fills us with sure hope all the while we suffer in this life, and so we are not defeated by tragic experiences, even the sudden loss of people we love more than life itself. Instead, we remain convinced that God can redeem this too. This is not the end because the beginning is always beginning, and what appears to be the end is precisely the beginning. The saints showcase a strange savor for a hidden sweetness found only in suffering: "For I resolved to know nothing while I was with you except Jesus Christ, and him crucified" (1 Cor 2:2). Writing to her mother while suffering severely from Addison's disease, Saint Elizabeth of the Trinity attests to the meaningfulness of redemptive suffering: "I'm keeping a rendez-vous with you in the shadow of the Cross to learn the science of suffering."[22] Similarly, in one of her originally composed retreats, she writes of the saint that "she no longer suffers from suffering."[23] And here again, a 1965 poem of American Discalced Carmelite Miriam of the Holy Spirit (Jessica Powers) entitled "Suffering" communicates this sentiment as well:

> She asked no more than that, beneath unwelcome,
> I might be mindful of her grant of grace.
> I still can smile, amused, when I remember
> how I surprised her when I kissed her face.[24]

For the disciple of Christ, the real test of authenticity is whether or not the fruits of the Holy Spirit are observable in the disciple's life.[25] Like so many things in the order of nature, as observed perceptibly by Aristotle, virtue most often is exercised as an avoidance of extremes and an achievement of the golden mean. This, too, is an important point for Carmelite spirituality when it comes to suffering and penitential practices. It is possible to take oneself too seriously and thereby to be filled with debilitating scrupulosities and anxieties. However, Jesus says to us in the Gospels: "Do not worry about your life" and "Come to me, all you who labor and are burdened, and I will give you rest. Take my yoke upon you and learn from me,

22. Elizabeth of the Trinity, *Complete Works,* 2:333.

23. Elizabeth of the Trinity, *Complete Works,* 1:147.

24. Powers, *Selected Poetry,* 106.

25. See Gal 5:22–23, and, especially pertinent to the topic at hand, Gal 5:24: "Now those who belong to Christ Jesus have crucified their flesh with its passions and desires." See also Matt 7:20: "So by their fruits you will know them."

for I am meek and humble of heart; and you will find rest for yourselves. For my yoke is easy, and my burden light" (Matt 6:25, 11:28–30). With these admonitions of Christ in mind, we must conclude that the Carmelite is not to take himself or herself too seriously, to a degree to which there would be no room for enjoyment, recreation, relaxation, or socialization (especially for Secular Discalced Carmelites). Oftentimes the Carmelite can fall into the host of spiritual vices—for example, spiritual gluttony, spiritual pride, or spiritual lust—that can harm body and soul due to a misplaced spiritual extremism.[26] The problem with anxiety and over-scrupulosity is that, in effect, it divides the attentiveness of the soul across many distractions. Since the Carmelite charism is an intensification and concentration of the con-templative life, a constant vigilance of virtue is required that would prevent the Carmelite from becoming either too lax or too tense. It is like a sail that catches the wind with the perfect temperament (not too tight and not too loose) in order for the boat to whisk merrily through the water. It is like tuning the string of a guitar, creating neither too much tension (or the string may break) nor too much slack (or the string may not sound at all). It is like seasoning food with salt or some other spice, neither too much nor too little, lest the dish be ruined. At many points, the Carmelite must be reminded of this vital piece of advice: relax! The main point, after all, is not consternation, indignation, or perturbation, but the peace of Christ and resting in him as he rested in the stern of the boat besieged by the turbu-lence of the sudden squall at sea. Saint Teresa of Ávila puts it best: *Nada te turbe* (Let nothing disturb you).[27]

In unison with the Christian life in general, the Carmelite life involves a daily renunciation of sin in all of its masquerading forms laced with the hollow promises of pleasure. On any occasion that I were to give in to sin, even to the most cursory ones, I am not in such instances living in fidelity to Christian discipleship, let alone fidelity to my specified Carmelite voca-tion. The cross entails a constant renunciation of sin begun at the baptismal promises of the faithful. For this reason, the life of the Carmelite is filled with detachment, self-denial, mortification, denudation, and suffering. Yet it is not a sadomasochistic life. That is, the Carmelite does not regard pain and deprivation as a perverted form of pleasure. Suffering is not sought out for its own sake. Rather, suffering is endured for a time for the sake of its

---

26. See John of the Cross, *Ascent of Mount Carmel*, in *Collected Works*, III.17–45, 294–349; *Dark Night*, in *Collected Works*, I.1–7, 361–75.

27. Teresa of Ávila, *Collected Works*, 3:386.

redemptive potential and its eventual alleviation. Detachment and regular penitential practices are necessary in order for the body not to dominate the soul and for the soul to overcome its allegiance to so many idols in this world. It is simply the calculus of Christian conversion. It is a daily affair. As a fallen personal creature, purgation is the indispensable route to union with God the Father, God the Son, and God the Holy Spirit. The human nature is the privileged locus of cosmic salvation because it exists at the intersection of personal spiritual being (soul) and material being (body). For this reason, the incarnation of Jesus happened. Yet there would have been no incarnation without the paschal mystery, that is, the suffering, death, resurrection, and ascension of Jesus. And, at the same time, there would have been no paschal mystery without the prior incarnation of Jesus. Human flesh is the potency of redemptive and vicarious suffering—one for the other. Human flesh is the conduit of the eternal regenerating waters of the Holy Spirit. Human flesh is the necessary nexus through which the Lord of glory ransoms and reforms the universe.

Three key terms articulate the pattern of the cross, and they are known as the evangelical counsels: poverty, chastity, and obedience. When Carmelites make their final vows or promises, they pledge to live according to the evangelical counsels. These describe the shape of the life of Jesus. He was poor, he was chaste, and he was obedient to God the Father and to the call of his fellow man. In his *Spiritual Exercises*, Saint Ignatius of Loyola indicates well the twofold meaning of poverty: material poverty and spiritual poverty. To live in poverty is to live in admitted need. It is to live in radical dependence on an other-than-the-self. It is not to consider oneself to be self-sufficient. It is to view oneself as a beggar before God at all times. Evangelical poverty involves a decision for poverty. It is a voluntary poverty that pursues poverty with the result of becoming rich in the things of God. For Carmelite religious, it means renouncing all possessions of one's own. For secular Carmelites, it means this same decisive renunciation of possessions, yet nevertheless having to deal with earthly goods every day in a completely detached way. It is possessing yet not possessing.[28] In either

---

28. See 1 Cor 7:29–31: "I tell you, brothers, the time is running out. From now on, let those having wives act as not having them, those weeping as not weeping, those rejoicing as not rejoicing, those buying as not owning, those using the world as not using it fully. For the world in its present form is passing away." See also 2 Cor 6:8–10: "We are treated as deceivers and yet are truthful; as unrecognized and yet acknowledged; as dying and behold we live; as chastised and yet not put to death; as sorrowful yet always rejoicing; as poor yet enriching many; as having nothing and yet possessing all things."

case, the Carmelite is one who rejoices in simplicity and dispossession. To have nothing is to have all, and to have all is to have nothing. United with material poverty is spiritual poverty. Spiritual poverty—to be "poor in spirit" (Matt 5:3)—means to keep one's soul vacant of all would-be inhabitants save divinity. Poverty of spirit signifies the daily hollowing out of the soul so that it might be as an inn of hospitality for its divine Guest. For if I were already rich in spirit, where would there be room for the perpetual circulation of the Unity of the Father, the Son, and the Holy Spirit?

Based in its Latin root *carere* (to be without), the evangelical counsel of chastity means to live without attachment to created goods. As applied to religious life, it implies a renunciation of the good of marriage in order to be devoted without reservation or distraction to God alone. Chastity means self-mastery and self-control, since being without attachment enables one to be self-possessed, or better, to be possessed without hindrance by the divine Bridegroom. To call Jesus Lord means exactly this. Whether married or not married, chastity signals mastery over the sexual urge and its tending toward "the lust of the flesh" (1 John 2:16). Even Saint John of the Cross attests that "the angel of Satan," of which Saint Paul speaks, is "the spirit of fornication."[29] What is fornication? From its Latin root, *fornus* (arched or domed shape) or *fornix* (brothel), fornication refers to voluntary sex between an unmarried man and an unmarried woman. It is a perversion of worship, erecting an arched enclosure atop concealed wantonness. Fornication begins with the desire to do so, and this disordered affection is called lust. It insinuates the reduction of the other person to an object of use. Lust reduces the other person to an impersonal means to an impersonal end. Lust reduces the other person to a tableaux of body parts fit for consumption. Fornication is counterintuitive to the gospel of Jesus because the gospel of Jesus is all about restoring the full dignity and sacredness of persons that were compromised by sin. The spirit of Satan is the spirit of fornication: "A thief comes only to steal and slaughter and destroy" (John 10:10). In contrast, the chaste Jesus says, "I am the good shepherd. A good shepherd lays down his life for the sheep" (John 10:11). Chastity is the pathway to restoring the full dignity and sacredness of persons, as well as the supernatural anticipation of the perfect communal integrity of the eschatological life: "At the resurrection they neither marry nor are given in marriage but are like the angels in heaven" (Matt 22:30). Absolute union with God precludes the possibility (and need) of sexual intercourse since heaven

---

29. See 2 Cor 12:7; John of the Cross, *Dark Night*, in *Collected Works*, I.14.1, 393.

is where the Lord alone fulfills every desire of the heart. Exposing the evil of fornication in no way undermines the goodness of the conjugal act in this life. Indeed, the sacrament of marriage is necessary for understanding the grand metaphor of the conjugal relationship between Christ the Bridegroom and his church the bride, and the virginal and celibate form of the eucharistic self-gift between them. Because fornication reduces love to lust and the person to an object (thereby destroying the integrity of the conjugal act), it has no place in the life of the follower of Christ. Chastity renounces the spirit of fornication and the temptation to lust that would reduce the person to an impersonal means to an impersonal and dehumanizing end. The cross of Jesus empowers chastity and quenches the destructive, futile fires of lust.

Obedience is the third evangelical counsel and refers to the yearning for the food of Jesus: "My food is to do the will of the one who sent me and to finish his work" (John 4:34). How do we know the will of God the Father unless we listen for it? Rooted in the most central Jewish concept of *shema* (to hear, listen, obey), obedience is the door of faith to the degree that "faith comes from what is heard" (Rom 10:17).[30] Obedience is a prerequisite for recognizing the voice of God and responding faithfully to his call comprised of a missionary itinerary of lifelong discipleship. For Carmelite religious life, obedience is lived out practically by submitting to the decisions and directives of one's superiors in the order. This concrete manifestation of obedience is intended to reflect the obedience of the human will to the will of God the Father as communicated through the word of Christ: "and what is heard comes through the word of Christ" (Rom 10:17). For Secular Discalced Carmelites, obedience is lived out in a constant attentiveness to divine providence, thereby knowing how to handle all of the day's demands according to the will of God the Father in resolute fidelity and responsibility. Obedience says with the prophet Elijah: *Zelo zelatus sum pro Domino Deo exercituum* (With zeal I have been zealous for the LORD, the God of hosts)! And with Jesus: "Zeal for your house will consume me" (John 2:17).[31] Obedience zealously listens for Christ's teachings, for the other's needs, and for the indications that point to the will of God the Father. Because obedience listens, the ears hear and the heart receives. There is no other way

---

30. See Deut 6:4–5: "Hear, O Israel! The LORD is our God, the LORD is one! Therefore, you shall love the LORD, your God, with your whole heart, and with your whole being, and with your whole strength."

31. See 1 Kgs 19:10, 14; Ps 69:10.

for the intentions of the Lord to be known aside from the way of steady obedience.

In his first epistle, Saint John writes, "Do not love the world or the things of the world. If anyone loves the world, the love of the Father is not in him. For all that is in the world, the lust of the flesh, the lust of the eyes, and the pride of life, is not from the Father but is from the world. Yet the world and its enticement are passing away. But whoever does the will of God remains forever" (1 John 2:15–17). The evangelical counsels counter these vicious tendencies of the flesh that, if left unchecked, would lead to mortal sin and eternal separation from God. Moreover, in a more contemporary profile, the analyses of human nature made by the so-called "masters of suspicion" (as dubbed by Paul Ricoeur), namely Karl Marx, Friedrich Nietzsche, and Sigmund Freud, also are refuted by the evangelical counsels. The "lust of the flesh" and the Freudian reductionism to libido are overcome by chastity. The "lust of the eyes" and the Marxian reductionism to mammon are surmounted by poverty. And the "pride of life" and the Nietzschean reductionism to the will to power are inverted by obedience. The Discalced Carmelites, like virtually all Christian religious orders, live according to the evangelical counsels that define the character of the Christ-life. Yet what is unique about the Carmelite charism is that these evangelical counsels are lived out especially through the apostolate of contemplation and a cloistered cruciform life in relation to the world. For the Carmelite, the dark night of contemplation envelops the soul as a happy and hidden horticulture of spirit.

4

Love and the Spousal Meaning
of the Body

I. THE MEANING OF LOVE

> *A la tarde te examinarán en el amor; aprende a amar como Dios*
> *quiere ser amando y deja tu condición.*
> In the evening (of life) you will be examined in love; learn to love
> as God wants to be loved and leave behind your condition.

John of the Cross, *Sayings of Light and Love*[1]

FOR THE CARMELITE, AND for every follower of Jesus Christ, love is the only thing, because love is everything. Love. There is no greater verb, there is no more essential vocation for a created person, whether human or angelic. Even Saint John the Apostle writes that "God is love (*agápe*), and whoever remains in love remains in God and God in him" (1 John 4:16). In its essence, love means the self-giving and other-receiving of persons in communion with one another, in the fullness of their integrity of being. It is the gaze and listening ear that affirms the other in his or her fundamental goodness of being and of being-in-relation to God who is Goodness itself. It is the refusal to use the other person as a means to an end, but always to regard the other person as the ultimate goal of action in himself or herself. Jesus, God in the flesh, shows us the meaning of love in every gesture, word,

---

1. John of the Cross, *Sayings of Light and Love*, in *Collected Works*, 90, line 59 (Spanish version), line 60 (English version). Translation my own.

46

movement, act, and signification of his. As we encounter him in his Gospels, in his church, and in his creation, we are met with a saturation of love and the ensuing recognition that all is gift, and, therefore, all is healable and redeemable. Jesus speaks divine love and shows divine love in the Eucharist. And this is the liturgy of the church: Jesus making himself present and proximate to us in word and sacrament. The liturgy, and the Eucharist himself, is where we come near to the God who has come near to us: "the love of God in Christ Jesus our Lord" (Rom 8:39).

Love is less an idea and more an experience, an event, a circulation of God the Holy Spirit who is Love beyond eternity and creation, yet who awakens both of these. Above all, Love is a divine Person: the Holy Spirit. God the Holy Spirit, *vinculum amoris* (the bond of love), gives being to beings and life to living beings. Proceeding eternally (and from beyond eternity) from God the Father and God the Son, God the Holy Spirit is the divine Wind who is destined to fill the spiritual sails of created finite spirits (angels) and souls (humans). A sail serves not its purpose without receiving the generous wind in its sheet and stay. When a sail receives its wind, it in turn propels its vessel to destinations purposeful and beautiful, and the voyage itself is wonderful. We use many analogies to think about God the Holy Spirit that are taken from the Scriptures and the inspired authors' contemplation of the natural order of creation: Wind, Breath, Water, Fire, Cloud, Chrism Oil, Power, Dove, and Gift. For us human beings, to love first means to receive the divine Gift of the Holy Spirit, and to adore this Gift and to share this Gift with the world. We love God with the Love that God is. We love other people with the Love that God is. Though Love does not originate with our finite created selves, Love loves to love through our gifted love that circulates to the measure that our wills are united with the will of God the Father. And the will of God the Father is made known to us through his Son and their Spirit. As the Catholic Church teaches, whenever the Father sends his Word, he always sends his Breath.[2] Love is both intelligible and affective.

Love signifies the unity of the Platonic transcendentals: truth, goodness, and beauty. When we experience divine Love (for there is no other love worthy of the name), we sense the unity of these transcendentals toward which all of our desires aim. Love is true. Love is good. Love is beautiful. We experience the truth of love when we are met with no greater intellectual and rational certainty. We experience the goodness of love when all of our

2. See John Paul II, *Catechism*, 689.

moral striving finally finds its rest and reason for being. We experience the beauty of love when every feeling and emotion is integrated according to a peaceful disposition of perfect affective fulfillment. Altogether, the unity of truth, goodness, and beauty is called happiness. It is a philosophical way of describing our supreme and unrivaled goal as human beings. Put in a theological tenor, as made known through God's self-revelation, complete communion with the Most Holy Trinity and all the angels and saints is our universal Destination Happiness. And from a Carmelite perspective, what we are describing is the mystical ascent of the soul en route to the summit of Mount Carmel: "In fact the goal of the 'ascent' is a condition in which all aspects of the human subject, including the body, are brought into harmonious relationship with one another, a condition which John (of the Cross) compares with that of Adam in Paradise . . . . Though there are certain periods of religious development in which the individual seems to be regressing or becoming more 'fragmented,' the overall movement is toward complete psycho-physical integration."[3] Or, as Saint Teresa of Ávila insists, love is never idle. It is either ascending or descending, either expanding or contracting. Love circulates in ascending and dilating fashion, or it is not love at all. Love causes a perfect harmonious integration of body and soul for the human person. Dissimilarly, when we sin, we experience a debilitating fragmentation and disintegration of body and soul and their relationship to one another. In the spiritual life, there is the negative fragmentation of sin that disunifies body and soul on the one hand, and, in complete contrast, the fragmentation of fragmentation (or reintegration) of repentance and sacramental healing that restores the unity of body and soul on the other hand. The unity of the body and the soul corresponds with the unity of truth, goodness, and beauty within the human experience.

"The kingdom of heaven is like a treasure buried in a field, which a person finds and hides again, and out of joy goes and sells all that he has and buys that field" (Matt 13:44). The love of God is this most mysterious buried treasure. It remains beneath the surface of objects and things. It is worth more than a universe of objects and things. Physics cannot measure it. Biology cannot dissect it. Chemistry cannot discover it through the periodic table of elements. Nevertheless, through the Incarnation, divine Love has a face and a name: Jesus Christ. In the incarnate Word is revealed the Breath of God the Father and God the Son—the Breath who is, at the same time, the uncreated Love of God the Father and God the Son, namely, God

3. Payne, *John of the Cross*, 19.

the Holy Spirit. Carmelite contemplation is, above all, a contemplation of the Love who is the unity of Persons of the Most Holy Trinity. The Carmelite vocation is to contemplate the Most Holy Trinity so as to enter into the mystery of divine Love by letting divine Love enter and remain in residence in the interior castle of the soul. More than anything else, love loves to love. The love between a husband and wife is a sacramental sign of this contemplative love that stretches toward an eternal rendezvous of loving. When a man and a woman sense the call to marriage, in the most authentic way, they share the desire to be together as much as possible. They want to tarry all day long together because they enjoy being in the presence of the other so much. They enjoy keeping company together. Whether it is getting ice cream, taking a walk in a park, going for a bike ride, sitting in solitude, listening to music, playing a game, washing the dishes, taking a trip, or even sleeping next to one another, husband and wife find great peace in one another's presence. The sacrament of marriage is meant to serve as an icon of the soul's relationship with God—the Church the Bride's relationship with Jesus the Bridegroom. God created the human soul for love. Love is the most foundational vocation of the soul. To love is to be human all the way, because God is love, and it is in his image that we are made.[4]

The Carmelite soul contemplates love, because love, above all, is worthy of contemplation. By contemplating love, the Carmelite soul loves God and other souls. From the Sacred Heart of Jesus divine Love flows. With reference to Saint Paul's analogy of the human body for understanding the church (see 1 Cor 12), the Carmelites could be thought of as the heart of the church. Their apostolate is not so much an active one that might be represented as the hands and the feet of the body, going here and there to minister to the world, such as that of the mendicant Orders. The Carmelite apostolate, much like that of the Benedictine monastics, is rather stable and stationary. For the Carmelite, the whole world comes to the window of the soul day and night. The Carmelite need not go so many places to contemplate love and to love the world to the throne of grace. This contemplation of love can be done anywhere, and the preferred place of contemplative prayer is one of hiddenness, silence, and solitude. Within Carmelite contemplation, the front country (the city) and the back country (the wilderness) meet. A Carmelite is able to contemplate just as well on a busy city street in comparison to the still enclosure of the monastic cell or the mountain

4. See Gen 1:27, 5:1, 9:6; Ps 8:6; Wis 2:23; Sir 17:3; Matt 19:4; Mark 10:6; Rom 8:29; 2 Cor 3:17–18, 4:4; Col 1:15, 3:10; James 3:9.

top. In either case, it is the soul that is essential, and the soul is not bound to any particular geometric coordinates in space-time. The prayerful soul can remain prayerful wherever she finds herself. Nevertheless, we might speak of a complementarity between city and wilderness inasmuch as both are needed to cultivate missionary contemplation. Without the city, contemplation would not be missionary in character; without the wilderness, contemplation would falter in its orientation around divinity. Like the heart of the body, Carmelites function in the church as those prayer warriors who serve to pump the precious blood of Christ through the veins of the entire mystical body of the church. For the Carmelite prays: "O Lord, may you love your world through me!"

If contemplation is the pinnacle of human activity, and if contemplation is the heart of all of the church's activity in the world, does it not make sense that some members of the global church would be dedicated to the apostolate of full-time contemplation? So much to contemplate and so little time! Love at its finest—divine Love—not only invites contemplation but lovingly demands it. It is only fitting to linger in perpetual contemplation over "what marvels the LORD worked for us!" (Ps 126:3). Love gives rise to contemplation, and, where love is ever loving, contemplation is ever rising. The contemplative is always beginning and never finishing. There is no point at which we will finish contemplating our incomprehensible, hidden, and yet revealed God. God always gives more to contemplate, for God never ceases to give himself to his beloved children. Since "the LORD's acts of mercy are not exhausted" and "his compassion is not spent" and his acts of mercy "are renewed each morning" (Lam 3:22–23), so is the vocation to contemplate renewed each morning and night. The Carmelite loves Love and so loves to contemplate Love without end. While it is not unprofitable to contemplate love as the best of abstract concepts, the Carmelite concentrates his or her contemplation on the heights of divine Love as revealed through the course of salvation history. The Carmelite delights in contemplating the saving works of God, especially "the love of God in Christ Jesus our Lord" (Rom 8:39), for this love has a face and a name—a revelation of the God who makes all things possible (see Matt 19:26). The Carmelite rejoices to contemplate the life of Jesus Christ by studying the Scriptures and the living Tradition of the church.

Love demands all because love gives all. Carmel is the garden of total self-giving through the active passivity that emulates the Blessed Virgin Mary's *fiat* in response to divine Gift. Just as Mary offered her entire body and soul to become Mother of the Lord of the universe, the Carmelite imitates this Marian abandonment to the divine will and summons. Love realizes that there is nothing better than to give over every ounce of one's soul and body to their Source and Summit, the Lord of glory. The Carmelite soul becomes "a praise of glory" (Saint Elizabeth of the Trinity), living in absolute praise and thanksgiving to God who "has done great things for us!" (Ps 126:3). Just as flowers open their buds and glorify God simply by staying stationary and rooted in their soil, the Carmelite opens her soul to the Light that is Christ and so glorifies him by reflecting his light with sweet fragrance and brilliant color.

II. THE HUMAN BODY: ARCHITECTURE OF DIVINE LOVE

Carmelite self-gift is actualized in both soul and body. In light of Pope Saint John Paul II's theological masterpiece the *Theology of the Body*, which contemplates the truth and meaning of the human body through the lens of divine revelation, this section of chapter 4 will reflect on the sacramental theology of the body and how the human body as male and female mediates the interpersonal itinerary of divine Love. It is important to remember that Carmelite contemplation is not a Platonic taking flight from the body and matter. Instead, Carmelite contemplation, as mentioned above, involves a complete harmonious integration of soul and body so that we might glorify God in our bodies (see 1 Cor 6:20). By contemplating nature as creation and the human body as the centerpiece of the order of created nature, the Carmelite moves to contemplate the full humanity of Christ, soul and body, united to his uncreated divinity. Carmelite spirituality is not a form of spiritualism that would disdain the material order of creation, including the human body and sexuality. Rather, Carmelite spirituality is a sacramental spirituality that contemplates things of spirit by way of things of matter. The Carmelite is attentive to the eucharistic sacramentality of creation, and the human body is the privileged locus of this sacramental encounter.

God created the human body in magnificent fashion. As the natural sciences reveal, through the evolutionary processes that God set in motion in the natural order of creation, the human body showcases the architecture of divine Love. When we contemplate the mystery of the Word made flesh, we find ourselves in awe that the being that God intended, before the dawn of creation, to unite with himself in an irrevocable way, is that of our own: human being.[5] And what are we if not soul and body? Here we concentrate our analysis on the body, never forgetful of its unity with the soul. In sacramental fashion, the visible and tangible body reveals the invisible and intangible soul. The spiritual is manifest in and through the material. Even though the flesh oftentimes can be at war with the spirit, Catholic doctrine never disowns the flesh as such. Although the language of the flesh sometimes is used to signify the inimical tendencies of concupiscence and the lingering effects of sin on the body especially, Catholic teaching treats the human body with great dignity: the eternal Son of God took a body to himself through his hypostatic union with the human nature (body and soul). Therefore, the Carmelite has good cause for contemplating the human soul and even the divine nature of Jesus in and through the human body.

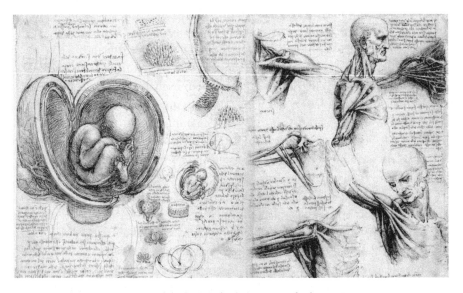

Among the sketches of the human body by Leonardo da Vinci, circa 1511.

The human body is incredibly beautiful in its simple unity of being and in its intricate plurality of parts. Contemporary anatomy and physiology acknowledge eleven different systems of the body that make up its totality. At the interior of the body is the skeletal system that gives the overall structure of the body, including joints and cartilage that enable movement.

5. See Wallenfang, *Human and Divine Being*, and Wallenfang, "From Albert Einstein to Edith Stein."

Connected immediately to the skeletal system is the muscular system that also functions to promote movement of the body and to aid other body systems in their functions. The nervous system, as command-control of the body, integrates all sense stimuli (sight, hearing, taste, touch, and smell) and signals muscular contraction and relaxation. The brain, as one of the most central organs of the body, is the site of thought and memory integration. The circulatory and respiratory systems serve to supply vital oxygen to all the body's organs and to transfer waste products (such as carbon dioxide) out of the body. The renal system, centered in the kidneys, filters the blood to extract waste products. The immune system (including the lymphatic organs, tissues, and fluid) guards the body against destructive pathogens. The endocrine system, comprised of the major endocrine glands such as the thyroid gland and the pancreas, functions to regulate hormone secretion that affects the operation of other organs in the body. The digestive system, including the main excretory organs, works to absorb necessary nutrients for metabolism and discards unnecessary waste products from the body. The integumentary system, including the exocrine glands, consists of the most exterior parts of the body (such as skin, hair and nails) that protect the body's interior and complete its formal material structure in space vis-à-vis other bodies and its local environment. Finally, the reproductive system, made up of the reproductive organs respective to the male and the female forms of the body, provide the ability of the human species to reproduce its kind through the sexual unification of the male body and the female body.

Is not the architecture of the human body so incredible and fascinating? When we take only a little time to contemplate our bodily composition, do we not find ourselves in a place of awe and wonder, yearning to praise the One responsible for such incredible design? And how the body is so instructive for the spiritual life and for understanding the mystical body of Christ that is the church! For all of the systems of the body are integrated together as a collective whole. Each system is completely dependent upon the others, forming a symbiotic, organic, and interdependent unity of individual being. Moreover, in relation to one another, individual human bodies are inherently collaborative and interdependent as well. We cannot survive and thrive without one another: "Now the body is not a single part, but many . . . . But as it is, God placed the parts, each one of them, in the body as he intended. If they were all one part, where would the body be? . . . But God has so constructed the body as to give greater honor to a part that is without it, so that there may be no division in the body, but that the parts may have the same concern for one another. If one part suffers, all the parts suffer with it; if one part is honored, all the parts share its joy" (1 Cor 12:14, 18–19, 24–26). In order to live, the human body must maintain homeostasis through the host of dynamic processes that regulate nutrition and waste; activity and rest; growth, development, and reproduction. The body is witnessed to circulate inwardly and outwardly. In a fallen world, we cannot live without dealing with spiritual pathogens and waste products that must be excised and exorcised in order to promote the full health of body and soul. These spiritual pathogens and waste products include demons, the concupiscent tendencies of the flesh, and the allurements of the world that trap a person in a life of profligacy, prodigality, and dissipation.[6] Through the communal and sacramental life of the church, by the power and grace of God at work within us, we are rid of these spiritual pathogens and waste products. We become more discerning and can distinguish better what is of God and what is not: "Beloved, do not trust every spirit but test the spirits to see whether they belong to God, because many false prophets have gone out into the world" (1 John 4:1). Carmelites, in the hidden garden of Carmel, fire the church with the love of the Father and of the Son by conducting the precious blood of Christ through the veins of the entire church by way of their silent yet sociable apostolate of contemplative prayer. This is a premier enactment of the spousal meaning of the human body and of the mystical body of Christ: total self-donation to the point of abandonment, body and soul, out of love for the Church and her divine Bridegroom.

So, what does all of this mean at the practical level of daily Carmelite living? While Carmelite spirituality (or Christian discipleship in general) does not advocate a "cult of the body," a Carmelite seeks to integrate body and soul as the effective unity of the human nature.[7] Even a suffering body, whether by involuntary illnesses and injuries or by voluntary penitential practices, can be a healthy contemplative body. Saint Paul writes:

> Do you not know that the runners in the stadium all run in the race, but only one wins the prize? Run so as to win. Every athlete exercises discipline in every way. They do it to win a perishable crown, but we an imperishable one. Thus I do not run aimlessly; I do not fight as if I were shadow boxing. No, I pommel my body

6. See John of the Cross, "The Precautions," in *Collected Works*, 720–24.
7. See John Paul II, *Catechism*, 2289.

and subdue it, lest after preaching to others I myself should be disqualified. (1 Cor 9:24–27)

Because of its constant struggle against concupiscence, the body needs to be mastered by the soul filled with the Love of God in order to cooperate with the spiritual itinerary of ascending Mount Carmel. Without falling into penitential extremism and thereby causing harm to body and soul, the Carmelite tempers penitential practices, all the while exercising them to their maximum potential. Proceeding from a contemplative disposition, Carmelites inevitably delight in the natural environment that surrounds them. They ponder the meanings that God has imbued in the natural order of creation: wind, water, sky, stars, planets, animals, plants, mushrooms, and all living and non-living beings. They also ruminate on angelic beings and the purity and intellectual superiority of their non-corporeal finite spiritual being as individual created spirits. While admitting that "the world is thy ship and not thy home" (Saint Thérèse of Lisieux), Carmelites do experience a sense of being at home in their own skin and enveloped by the beauty of nature. We are reminded of how Saint John of the Cross greatly enjoyed walks through the countryside as a means of facilitating higher degrees of contemplative prayer—or even how he enjoyed eating asparagus (without letting it become an edible idol in his heart or stomach)!

Carmelites may enjoy physical exercise, a savory cup of coffee, a tasty meal, or an edifying conversation with a friend, while not bowing down to worship any of these gifts, precisely because they regard them as gifts from their Creator, and, in turn, worship and thank their Creator all the more. For the Carmelite, because of her childlike perception and imagination, the world lights up as a polyphony of gifts calling out to the gifted contemplative beneficiary of all that God gives. Carmelites render praise to whom it is due and hold very loosely to the things of the world. They are able to live as Saint Paul suggests: "Let those having wives act as not having them, those weeping as not weeping, those rejoicing as not rejoicing, those buying as not owning, those using the world as not using it fully. For the world in its present form is passing away. I should like you to be free of anxieties" (1 Cor 7:29–32). Whether religious or secular Carmelites, a spirit of detachment prevails vis-à-vis all created and temporary goods. It is a mysterious paradox that body and soul flourish to the measure that we both enjoy what the Lord has made and deny ourselves many enjoyments along the way for the sake of adoring our gracious God and ensuring the good of the other human beings facing us.

5

The Blessed Virgin Mary

A queen arrayed in the gold of Ophir comes to stand at your right hand.

Ps 45:10

AROUND THE TURN OF the thirteenth century, a small remnant of Christian soldiers established a new contemplative monastic community on Mount Carmel in the land of Israel, calling themselves the Order of the Brothers of the Blessed Virgin Mary of Mount Carmel. A book cannot be written on Carmelite spirituality without dedicating at least one chapter to Our Lady, for she is the Mother and model of the contemplative life. Mary is the very beauty of Carmel, and perfect contemplation is the Marian life. In order to ponder the "Mary-form life," I will comment on four key biblical passages that illuminate her paradigmatic Carmelite character.[1]

1. See Paul-Marie of the Cross, *Carmelite Spirituality*, 29. Cf. 28–30: "*Totus marianus est* . . . (Mary) represents and expresses the soul's essential attitude before God . . . [the] Marian attitude of virginal simplicity and pure reference to God. In Carmel God is the objective, but the soul will become more and more Mary."

I. "AND MARY KEPT (*SYNTERÉO*) ALL THESE THINGS, REFLECTING (*SYMBÁLLO*) ON THEM IN HER HEART (*KARDÍA*)" (LUKE 2:19).

Why is Mary the model contemplative? Because she keeps all of the mysteries of the life of her Son within her and before her, reflecting on them over and over again in her heart. Saint Luke's inspired choice of words, here in the context of the pastoral visitation and adoration surrounding the nativity of Jesus, are much deeper than any single English translation can render them. The Greek word *synteréo* can mean "to keep," but it also can mean "to protect, keep safe, preserve, keep in good condition, remember, or treasure up." Mary never ceases, even for an instant, to savor and ruminate upon the wealth of mysteries of divine revelation that were entrusted to her more than to any other creature. By keeping these precious recollections safe within the interior fortress of her soul, Mary, the Immaculate Conception, is united completely and without flaw with the Most Holy Trinity. To the extent that she protects what has been entrusted to her, what has been entrusted to her protects her. For what has been committed and confided to Mary by God is the invaluable and exorbitant elixir that is ordained to redeem the entire cosmos. There is nothing that compares to the worth of the Word of God become flesh in her. And so we worship him alongside his Mother, who began worshipping him without deviation from the time of her undefiled conception onward. Mary's anamnestic memory is the basis of the church's liturgical *memoria*, for she is the Mother of the church. Mary refuses to forget (*an-amnesia*, forgets not) the saving works of God that have taken place within her. She treasures up the storehouse of divine treasures like a thesaurus (*thesaurós*, treasure store, treasure box, storeroom) that hosts a treasury of words that open the world of meaning and meaningfulness.

Not only does Mary "keep all these things" in her contemplative memory, she also "reflects on them in her heart." Again, the Greek language employed by Saint Luke is fraught with meaning. The Greek word *symbállo* can be translated "to reflect," but it likewise can be rendered "to meet, encounter, discuss, confer, debate, help, assist, think about, or consider." The Greek word *symbállo* is the root of the English word symbol. *Symbállo* literally means "to throw or crash together." In her heart, Mary allows the parabolic mysteries of faith to collide and therein generate a plethora of doctrinal truths and daily liturgical acts of worship. And closely related to the Greek word *symbállo* is the word *syllambáno* (to seize, become pregnant, or catch [fish]). In other words, Mary's heart (soul), as well as her womb, is pregnant with divine life. When we contemplate Mary contemplating divinity, we study the cardiology of Carmelite contemplation. In her heart, Mary encounters her Lord and Savior and Teacher, who is at once her Son, at every turn—which is to say, never turning away from him and his redemptive gaze: "The Lord will give you bread in adversity and water in affliction. No longer will your Teacher hide himself, but with your own eyes you shall see your Teacher, and your ears shall hear a word behind you: 'This is the way; walk in it,' when you would turn to the right or the left'" (Isa 30:20–21).[2] Further, since Mary has been caught by divine grace, she is the exemplar "fisher of men" in how her heart, like that of her Son, is filled with faces and names. Beneath the beating heart of the Blessed Virgin Mary is the beating sacred heart of Jesus. Because his heart beats with an imperishable Love, so does hers. In her immaculate heart, Mary encounters the sacred heart of her Son and his unquenchable merciful love for sinners. It is the immaculate heart of Mary that accompanies the sacred heart of Jesus in his insuperable love for the world: "For God did not send his Son into the world to condemn the world, but that the world might be saved through him" (John 3:17). In a paradoxical way, Mary discusses and debates with God in the secret chambers of her heart.[3] From its Latin root *battere* (to bat), the word debate signifies batting something for an extended period of time in order to get at the heart of the matter. We might

2. Cf. Deut 4:39, 5:32–33: "This is why you must now acknowledge, and fix in your heart, that the LORD is God in the heavens above and on earth below, and that there is no other. . . . Be careful, therefore, to do as the LORD, your God, has commanded you, not turning aside to the right or to the left, but following exactly the way that the LORD, your God, commanded you that you may live and prosper, and may have a long life in the land which you are to possess." Prov 4:25–27: "Let your eyes look straight ahead and your gaze be focused forward. Survey the path for your feet, and all your ways will be sure. Turn neither to the right nor to the left, keep your foot far from evil." Gen 3:15: "I will put enmity between you and the woman, and between your offspring and hers; they will strike at your head, while you strike at their heel."

3. See Luke 1:34: "But Mary said to the angel, 'How can this be, since I have no relations with a man?'" Luke 2:33–35: "The child's father and mother were amazed at what was said about him; and Simeon blessed them and said to Mary his mother, 'Behold, this child is destined for the fall and rise of many in Israel, and to be a sign that will be contradicted (and you yourself a sword will pierce) so that the thoughts of many hearts may be revealed.'" Luke 2:48: "When his parents saw him, they were astonished, and his mother said to him, 'Son, why have you done this to us? Your father and I have been looking for you with great anxiety.'" John 2:3: "When the wine ran short, the mother of Jesus said to him, 'They have no wine.'"

think of a *piñata* that, when struck, gushes forth with hidden saccharine treasures. Just as Israel "wrestles with God," and just as a farmer beats the harvest on the threshing floor to separate the wheat from the chaff, so does Mary pore over the mysterious works of God that fill and envelop her life.[4]

Like Mary, the Carmelite is called "to keep (*syntereo*) all these things, reflecting (*symbállo*) on them in her heart (*kardía*)." This was the original intention of "Brother B." and his companions when they set up their hermitage on Mount Carmel in the late twelfth century: to stay, watch, and pray with Mary as sentinels of the church for the salvation of souls. A Carmelite remains steadfast in prayer in his monastic cloistered cell as a reflection of the prayerful hidden constancy of the cell of his soul. He has no greater delight than "to meditate day and night on the Law of the Lord and to keep watch in prayer." A Carmelite stays at the side of Christ with contemplative adoring vigilance like Moses, who lets not his arms grow weary lest Israel grow faint in the fight.[5] A Carmelite's heart beats in tandem with the rhythm of the sacred heart of Jesus without cardiac arrest. Just as a heart beats on so that the body stays alive, Carmelites pray on so that the divine Breath has its effect circulating throughout the mystical body of Christ, that is, the church. And just as the heart beats faster in times of exercise, elation, or distress, and beats slower during times of relaxation and rest, so does the heart of the Carmelite pulsate according to its diastolic and systolic meter that is both contemplative and missionary in its essence, after the pattern of the sacred heart of Jesus. Whatever arises in a time of need, the Carmelite heart beats accordingly at the service of sacred mediation on behalf of those sheep who have gone missing or are undergoing suffering. Like Mary, the Carmelite heart is attentive to the cries of the children of God. Saint Teresa of Jesus compares Mary, our humble Queen Mother, to the most powerful piece in the game of chess, the queen: "There's no queen like humility for making the King surrender. Humility drew the King from heaven to the womb of the Virgin, and with it, by one hair, we will draw Him to our souls."[6] So let us call upon our Queen to be victorious in the

---

4. See Gen 32:22–33; Ruth 3:2–15; 2 Sam 24:16–25; 1 Kgs 22:10; 2 Chr 3:1; Isa 21:8–10; Joel 2:24; Matt 3:12.

5. See Exod 17:8–15.

6. Teresa of Ávila, *Way of Perfection*, in *Collected Works*, 2:16.1–2, 94: "Now realize that anyone who doesn't know how to set up the pieces for a game of chess won't know how to play well. And if he doesn't know how to check his opponent's king, he won't know how to checkmate it either . . . and how quickly, if we play it often, will we checkmate this divine King, who will not be able to escape, nor will He want to. The queen

contest, sacrificing whatever it might be to draw all souls into the sheepfold of Jesus the Good Shepherd.

II. "AND HIS MOTHER KEPT (*DIATERÉO*) ALL THESE THINGS IN HER HEART (*KARDÍA*)" (LUKE 2:51).

To reiterate the contemplative character of Mary, this time in the context of finding the twelve-year-old Jesus in the temple (a bar mitzvah event of sorts), Saint Luke once again highlights how Mary "kept all these things in her heart," using a different Greek word than that of the previous passage, *diateréo* (to keep, maintain, conserve, preserve, subsist, sustain, treasure up). From its root parts, *dia-téras* (consisting of a wonder, an object of wonder, an omen, or something indicating a coming event), *diateréo* suggests that Mary sustains contemplation of the wonders of the Lord in her heart. Mary is the prophetess of hope who houses and preserves her presage of mercy that will be poured out upon the house of Israel and the homeless Gentiles alike. As an elected augur of the most sublime mysteries of faith, Mary contemplates (*con-templum, con-tempus,* to be within the sacred space for observation marked out by an augur, or to be within the time of the temple) the great things the Mighty One has done for her.[7]

So does a Carmelite soul strive for this elected time and space of contemplating the "wondrous deeds" of the LORD (Ps 40:6). "In my heart I treasure your promise, that I may not sin against you" (Ps 119:11). The Carmelite protects the hidden treasure (*thesaurós*) that he found buried in a field and the pearl (*margarítes*) of great price for which he sold all he had in order to buy it.[8] The Carmelite, continually "instructed in the kingdom of heaven," avoids the near occasion of ideology by thinking, speaking, and acting "like the head of a household who brings from his storeroom both the new and the old" (Matt 13:52). A faithful Carmelite resists the temptation to quietism and antinomianism by abiding in the sacramental heart

---

is the piece that can carry on the best battle in this game, and all the other pieces help. There's no queen like humility for making the King surrender. Humility drew the King from heaven to the womb of the Virgin, and with it, by one hair, we will draw Him to our souls. And realize that the one who has more humility will be the one who possesses Him more; and the one who has less will possess Him less. For I cannot understand how there could be humility without love or love without humility; nor are these two virtues possible without detachment from all creatures."

7. See Luke 1:49.

8. See Matt 13:44–46.

of the church and remaining obedient to all of her magisterial teachings, never severing prayer from the demands of responsibility for the neighbor and the stranger. Carmelite spirituality is cultivated always under the mantle of Mary, since no one can enjoy full proximity to Jesus except through his grace-filled Mother. A Carmelite dwells not on Mount Carmel without "treasuring up all these things in her heart."

III. "WHEN THE WINE RAN SHORT (*HYSTERÉO*), THE MOTHER OF JESUS SAID TO HIM, 'THEY HAVE NO WINE.' . . . HIS MOTHER SAID TO THE SERVERS, 'DO (*POIÉO*) WHATEVER HE TELLS YOU'" (JOHN 2:3, 5).

A third biblical scene that brings us to the Carmelite charism on display in the Blessed Virgin Mary is the wedding feast at Cana in Galilee. Mary, Jesus, and Jesus's disciples were present there. The first interesting detail of this story is that Mary notices that the wine is running short. The Greek word used in Saint John's Gospel for "running short" is *hysteréo* (to lack, have need of, fall short of, be inferior to or less than, lacking apparent importance, give out, be worse off). Related to a similar Greek noun, *hystérema* (need, want, absence, poverty), *hysteréo* signifies the condition of possibility for Jesus to perform a miracle. Without a prior lack, there is nothing to fill. Without the state of poverty, there is nothing to be enriched. Without need or want, there is no gift to receive. Without being worse off, there is no need to become better off. Without inferiority, there is no occasion to be raised to superiority. Without a prior absence, there is no room for the advent of presence. Without being in hysterics, there is no evident crisis from which to cry out to God. While the *hysteréo* of wine seems like a bad thing at this wedding feast, it actually is the best thing that could have happened. For how would the guests ever have tasted the "good, fine, precious, and beautiful (*kalós*)" wine pressed by the Savior, had they not found themselves in dire need and in a place of humiliation? Further, how could the seed of the Word have been sown (*hys*) in the flesh without a receptive womb or uterus (*hystera*) become his incarnate home? Once again, *hystérema* (need, want, absence, poverty) is the condition of possibility for miraculous divine intervention. And what the Lord has proven to us is that he always will act on our behalf, bringing about our greater good, sooner or later. His timing is often not always our timing, but time is on God's side and you can be sure that he will work in your favor sooner or later. And when he does work, "then you shall see and be radiant, your heart shall throb and overflow. For the riches of the sea shall be poured out before you, the wealth of nations shall come to you" (Isa 60:5). Our God is the God of restoration and resurrection. We can trust his promise to save, to redeem, to heal, and to mend. Our God is the God who "makes all things new" (Rev 21:5).[9]

Next, following the plot of this story, Mary brings the poverty of wine to the attention of her Son, and, at the same time, commands the stewards, "Do whatever he tells you." These two details show forth the Carmelite charism in Mary. As Mother of the church, Mary desires the entire garden of Carmel to flourish. She is the master gardener, cultivating with care the fragile flowers and precious produce. She works to ensure that the soil is rich and properly irrigated, that the Son is shining upon the leaves of every plant, that weeds and pestilence do not destroy what "the right hand of the Lord has planted" (Ps 80:16). With steadfast devotion to the Blessed Virgin Mary, Carmelites abide in her most powerful intercession as they intercede through substitution on behalf of suffering sinners. Carmelites notice the many shortages that have evolved in culture, family life, and even in the church—the great fragmentation, dislocation, and disorientation that has occurred in the wake of so many revolutions that have affected social relationships at their core.[10] Carmelites dedicate themselves to acting as stewards of restoration of these relationships that are rooted in right relationship with God. Carmelites live in obedience to the command of Christ through the command of Mary: "Do (*poiéo*) whatever he tells you." They trust the voice of their beloved Mother, just as they trust the voice of their beloved Brother. Like her Son, Mary herself empowers the doing she commands, accomplishing the creative and saving works of God: "Blessed be the Lord, the God of Israel, for he has visited and brought redemption (*poiéo lútrosis*, to accomplish redemption or liberation) to his people" (Luke 1:68). The Carmelite wants to unite his doing (*poiéo*) to the doing (*poiéo*) of divinity, that these would be one. And by "doing whatever he tells you," miracles happen, and water is changed into wine, sooner or later.

9. Cf. Isa 43:18–19; Isa 65:17; Heb 8:13.
10. See Wallenfang, "*Cor quietum.*"

IV. "THE WOMAN HERSELF FLED (*PHEÚGO*) INTO THE DESERT WHERE SHE HAD A PLACE PREPARED (*HETOIMÁZO*) BY GOD, THAT THERE SHE MIGHT BE TAKEN CARE OF (*TRÉPHO*) FOR TWELVE HUNDRED AND SIXTY DAYS" (REV 12:6).

One final biblical passage assists us in our reflection on the Carmelite character of the Blessed Virgin Mary. This apocalyptic vision concerning Mary, originating with Saint John the Apostle, whom Jesus put in charge of caring for his Mother while they stood at the foot of the cross, discloses the Carmelite soul in relation to the persecutions of the world, the flesh, and the devil. Two of the perennial tasks of the Christian life are to renounce sin and to flee it: "If you do well, will you not be accepted? And if you do not do well, sin is crouching at the door; its desire is for you, but you must master it. . . . Flee from youthful passions and pursue righteousness, faith, love, and peace, along with those who call on the Lord out of a pure heart" (Gen 4:7; 2 Tim 2:22). "The woman herself fled (*pheúgo*) into the desert." Mary is described as fleeing, not out of cowardice, but out of necessity. She is a refugee on earth because the Immaculate Conception has no lasting home in cities of sin. As a model for the desert hermits of the early church, Mary flees into the desert because it is there that she could be "alone with the Alone" (Elizabeth of the Trinity). The Greek verb *pheúgo* means to flee, run away, escape, shun, turn from, disappear, vanish. Similar to the body and soul of her resurrected Son, the body and soul of Mary would vanish eventually from this world through her blessed assumption into heaven. She escapes the world, the flesh, and the devil by the grace of God manifest and proclaimed through her perpetual virginity of body and soul. She escapes the empty promises of pleasure by making the great escape, evacuation, and exodus of herself from herself. She takes leave of the egocentrism and fleshpots of Egypt in favor of the undying vocation of responsibility for the other. Mary is Mother of the church forever. She is Queen of heaven and earth because she exercises perfect responsibility for her subjects in the kingdom of God. She is the great Mediatrix of salvation because her very Son is the Savior.

Mary stays vigilant in the place prepared (*hetoimázo*) for her by God. The Lord makes ready (*hetoimázo*) a place for Mary, just as Mary had made ready a home in her heart for the Father, the Son, and the Holy Spirit: "My heart is ready, O God, my heart is ready. I will sing and chant praise. Awake, my soul; awake, lyre and harp. I will awake the dawn" (Ps 57:8–9).[11] And in this designated cloister and solitary hermitage, God takes care of her during the period of persecution. Just as the LORD fed the prototypical Carmelite Elijah with a hearth cake beneath the solitary broom tree during his escape from bloodthirsty Jezebel, the LORD "feeds, provides for, nourishes, sustains, supports, nurses, and raises up" (*trépho*) Mary and the Carmelite soul during their escape from the world, the flesh, and the devil, even while they "run and rush" (*trécho*) into the visitation of battle. Another paradox is noticeable here: escape and arrival in one and the same movement. The world, the flesh, and the devil are fled, only to be conquered in the end. The Carmelite escapes by entering the cloister of contemplative prayer, only to find herself on the frontline of battle against all that is opposed to Jesus Christ, the King of the universe. Carmel is at once a place of silence and riot, of solitude and sociality, of contemplation and ethics, of peace and war, of calm and storm, of light and darkness, of day and night. Yet this nighttime departure is precisely the noonday of accomplishing the divine will: "Joseph rose and took the child and his mother by night and departed for Egypt" (Matt 1:14). The Holy Family ventures to Egypt only to make a renewed exodus from there: "Out of Egypt I called my son" (Matt 1:15). In the Holy Family's flight to Egypt, we behold once again the Josephite and Marian life of discipleship in relation to their infant Son: to stand proxy for sinners, substituting oneself for the other in radical responsibility to the point of joyful abandonment.

---

11. Cf. Ps 45:2: "My heart is stirred by a noble theme, as I sing my ode to the King. My tongue is the pen of a nimble scribe."

6

Silence, Solitude, and Contemplation

At daybreak, Jesus left and went to a deserted place. . . . He would withdraw to deserted places to pray.

LUKE 4:42, 5:16

I. SILENCE AND SOLITUDE

SILENCE AND SOLITUDE ARE the necessary conditions of possibility for hearing the voice of God with greatest clarity. Without these, the soul hears only the babel of noises that drown out what the Lord would have to say within the intimate and incognito recesses of its inmost being. From its Latin root *sinere* (to leave, let go, lay), the word silence implies departure, surrender and rest. "Come away by yourselves to a deserted place and rest a while" (Mark 6:31). Silence and solitude go hand in hand for Carmelite spirituality. These two define the Carmelite environment. When the Carmelite is alone, she is not really alone. To be alone is to be in the best of divine company. The Carmelite prefers silence to music and prefers the windswept cliff to the crowd. It is not that Carmelites have contempt for things like concerts or large gatherings of people. Even these settings can lend themselves to meaningful contemplation and ethical opportunities to exercise love and responsibility. But to encounter the Most Holy Trinity in closest proximity, a Carmelite must take leave of the hustle and bustle of the multitudes, surrender everything, and find rest in the sacred heart of Jesus, away from the masses. In this sense, the sonorous city is brought into the silent chapel for the sake of its metamorphosis into the kingdom of God.

Traditionally, for cloistered Carmelites, since the foundation of the order, "the cell becomes the desert where the soul meets its God."[1] Reminiscent of Elijah's rendezvous with YHWH at the mouth of a desert cave, the cell of a Carmelite is the privileged place of YHWH passing by.[2] It is here, in silence and solitude, that the Carmelite recognizes her soul as a living tabernacle of the divine Presence. Renouncing all idols and withdrawing into her cloistered cell to bask in the quiescent light of prayer, the Carmelite outwardly expresses what is happening inwardly in her soul. Just as she dwells in a cell of which no other human being makes observation, God dwells in the cell of her soul without any outside witnesses. What God speaks and does in the solitary soul, no one else can know. How God moves in the individual soul, no one else can perceive. Again, the *Carmelite Rule of Saint Albert* advises: "Each one shall remain in his cell or near it, meditating day and night on the Law of the Lord and watching in prayer." Carmelites "instinctively cling to what is most simple and ordinary because that is what makes it possible for them to give themselves in peace to 'the one thing necessary.'"[3]

Unum necessarium—"the one thing necessary," "the pearl of great price," "the treasure hidden in a field." The life of the Carmelite orbits around this one thing necessary. "Martha, Martha, you are anxious and worried about many things. There is need of only one thing. Mary has chosen the better part and it will not be taken from her" (Luke 10:41–42). And this is the great secret of life: "there is need of only one thing" after all. The Carmelite discovers this secret anew every morning. Placing herself at the feet of Jesus to soak

1. Paul-Marie of the Cross, *Carmelite Spirituality*, 24.

2. See 1 Kgs 19:1–14.

3. Paul-Marie of the Cross, *Carmelite Spirituality*, 25. Cf. Von Balthasar, *Two Sisters in the Spirit*, 9–10: "For God does not give himself in Christ merely for the sake of a bit of dialogue and action among men and women, rather God eucharistically pours himself out endlessly in absolute love . . . . This forms the center of every Christian contemplative vocation, a vocation received first by the Mother of the Lord, who answered it with her own *Fiat!* Since her Son needs followers not only for the actions and organizations of his church, but to help complete his hidden position before the Father, there will always be a Mary who 'chooses the best part' and desires to live solely to hear and carry out the divine word. Far from being a flight from the world, Carmel and all purely contemplative forms of life in the church extrapolate the encounter between the world and the living God of Jesus Christ to its most radical point."

in his parabolic teachings that blaze a trail to "the one thing necessary" like a recurring melody of a symphony, the Carmelite gathers up the words that fall from his lips as a farmer gathers in the precious fruit of the harvest, or as the honeybees gather up the pollen and nectar to construct, preserve, and reinforce their secluded hive. To receive this one thing necessary requires a dormition of all perceptions, passions (joy, hope, fear, sorrow), and powers or faculties (intellect, memory, will) of the soul. This is why silence and solitude are absolutely necessary for the Carmelite way of prayer. Without these, the perceptions, passions, and powers of the soul cannot be quieted, hushed, stilled, and put to sleep. Without silence and solitude, too many sense stimuli occupy the soul, too many earthbound concerns weigh down the soul, too many emotions toss the soul about like a ship lumbering through a severe storm. And, as Saint John of the Cross shows, even the higher faculties of the soul—the intellect, the memory, and the will—must be emptied and stilled, as well as the unruly appetites of the body. One cannot embrace "the one thing necessary" apart from the dark night of the soul, and this dark night is accompanied always by silence and solitude.

In today's world, silence and solitude are quite difficult to come by. Where can a person go to find zero noises sounding in the ears, zero distractions tugging at the senses? It is a great challenge to find such a place, especially as a Secular Discalced Carmelite. Since ours is an age of saturating pollution, clamor, and so many virtual and digital worlds of being that distend the soul in every direction, we must labor tirelessly to reconnect with the elemental and reenter the truth that our being is bound up with the natural order of creation. When our ears are retuned to decipher the polyphony of the birds, when our eyes are reopened to the kaleidoscope of those beautiful forms of the visible, and when our bodies are reintroduced to the beneficent perceptions that intertwine with the flesh as a symbiotic communion of life and being, then we are disposed properly to the delightful and daring desensitization of the dark night. Only once you have seen the world can you un-see it. Only once you have heard the world can you un-hear it. Only once you have smelled the world can you un-smell it. Only once have you tasted the world can you un-taste it. Only once you have touched the world can you un-touch it. Only once you have understood the world can you de-understand it. Only once you have memorized the world can you de-memorize it. Only once you have willed the world can you de-will it. Following the paradigmatic structure of Christian mystical ascent, kataphatic assertions precede their respective apophatic denegations. The dark night of the soul follows affirmation of the inherent goodness of the created order of being. It is neither an annihilation of creation nor an idolization of it. Rather, we proceed to contemplate the beyond-the-good once we have taken time to become acquainted with the good. We advance to the mystical once we have been familiarized with the mundane. We tend toward the suprarational once we have learned the ropes of the rational. Altogether, one cannot climb the mountain without beginning at the bottom and elevating step by step. There is no *via negativa* of the dark night without a prior *via positiva* of noonday light. Spiritual and theological negations happen only in relation to their positive kataphatic correlates.

Silence and solitude predispose the soul to make the transition from the goodness of natural enjoyments—the enjoyment of the elemental and the simple pleasures of life—to the paradoxical illumination and mystical (otherworldly) contemplation of the dark night and, ultimately, divine union. For this reason, it is necessary for a Carmelite to validate created goods as divine gifts offered to their personal, created beneficiaries. Only then can the Carmelite prescind from the goodness of creatures to the super-goodness of the Creator—to the Love that "is older than these" and that "had no beginning."[4] Silence effects its full power once we have practiced the art of speaking and listening. Solitude renders the soul fruitful to the degree that we have affirmed our innate sociality as persons. For silence prepares the soul for the sonority of the divine Word, and solitude schools the soul for the fullness of fraternity in the communion of angels, saints, and the Most Holy Trinity. The ascent of Mount Carmel is an arduous trek that a former student humorously described as the ascent up "Mount Doom!" Nevertheless, "my grace is sufficient for you, for power is made perfect in weakness" (2 Cor 12:9), and "The LORD will fight for you; you have only to be silent and still" (Exod 14:14).

II. THE ART OF MYSTICAL CONTEMPLATION

> Jesus went up on the mountain by himself to pray.
> Matt 14:23

By this point in the book, it has been made clear that the charism and apostolate of Discalced Carmelites is contemplative prayer: "Contemplation is

---

4. See Jessica Powers's poem "For a Lover of Nature" in Powers, *Selected Poetry*, 165.

the heart of Carmel, its reason, its distinguishing mark, its protection."[5] But what exactly is contemplation, and how does it work? This section will lay out the art of mystical contemplation, differentiating it from other types of prayer, showing what it is and what it is not. Together we will examine the overall gestalt of the spiritual ascent of Mount Carmel, as well as each step along the way. We will compare the metaphors of the two dark nights of which Saint John of the Cross speaks to the interior castle and the various types of water in relation to the soul, as spoken of by Saint Teresa of Jesus. Central to our understanding of the sequential stages of Carmelite prayer is Saint Teresa of Jesus's five distinct categories of prayer. We will unearth all of these below, but first, let us consider the classic three general stages of spiritual ascent as featured in the tradition of Christian spirituality on the whole:

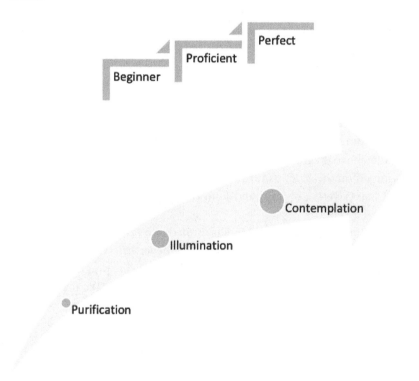

Perfect

Proficient

Beginner

Contemplation

Illumination

Purification

The Three Stages of Spiritual Ascent

As these two diagrams exhibit, there are three categories of prayerful souls: (1) the beginner who is engaged primarily in penitential practices of

5. Paul-Marie of the Cross, *Carmelite Spirituality*, 32.

purification, (2) the proficient who has ascended to the kataphatic wisdom of divine illumination, and (3) the perfect who has ascended to the apophatic forms of contemplation proper. As you can see, contemplation proper is the most advanced stage of the spiritual ascent. It is not what is happening during the earlier stages of the soul's journey to God, but it is the fruit of much time and effort expended in the stages of purification and illumination. This is not to say that the proficient or perfect are unconcerned with penitential practices. These of course continue throughout the course of this life. Yet this is to say that you must "pay your dues" through much self-denial, mortification, and detachment before you can ascend to the study of Scripture and Tradition in order to be lifted toward the peak of Mount Carmel's heights of contemplative prayer. Other terms for the summit of Mount Carmel are divinization, theosis, or union with God: "Beloved, we are God's children now; what we shall be has not yet been revealed. We do know that when it is revealed we shall be like him, for we shall see him as he is. Everyone who has this hope based on him makes himself pure, as he is pure" (1 John 3:2–3). To see God as he is ultimately refers to the beatific vision of heaven, but the furthest reaches of contemplative prayer in this life are a foretaste of this vision of the Lord of glory: "All of us, gazing with unveiled face on the glory of the Lord, are being transformed into the same image from glory to glory, as from the Lord who is the Spirit" (2 Cor 3:18). So, the above diagrams outline the general pathway of a soul en route to divine union. Now, let us turn to Mount Carmel more specifically and to what Saints Teresa of Jesus and John of the Cross have to say about this mystical ascent.

While the scope of this book is limited to a preliminary introduction to the Discalced Carmelite way of life, we nevertheless must make passing reference to the definite contours of the Carmelite progression toward contemplative prayer. To aid us in our discovery, let us take the Carmelite emblem as our visual model:

This is the symbol of Mount Carmel, or the soul's peregrination to God. The summit of the mountain is defined by the cross of Jesus Christ. Jesus is described as the mountain itself and, especially, he is identified as its summit, the great reward of the expedition involving not a little spiritual rigor. The single star shown on the mountain is the pilgrim soul on earth, making his or her way up the mountain by the grace of God. The two stars shown on either side of the cross represent those blessed souls who have ascended the mountain according to the successive stages of purification, illumination, and contemplation, and are now in the company of the angels and saints in heaven, united to the Most Holy Trinity in the perfection of their created being. This is the coat of arms of the Carmelites and a helpful image to remember while we trace the individual stages of the soul's spiritual sojourn on this side of eternity. We tend to imagine prayer as an experience as unique as each person whose soul cries out. We know it to be a rather fluid phenomenon with no real lines of division between one type of prayer and the next. There is much truth to this perception. However, the Carmelite saints present us with an explanation of prayer in different and distinct types, so that we may have a visual of the heart in motion. Now we shall consider Saint Teresa of Jesus's five stages of prayer as she discusses them across her written works: (1) vocal prayer, (2) mental prayer or meditation, (3) prayer of recollection, (4) prayer of quiet, and (5) prayer of union.[6] Here, we zoom in on the slope of Mount Carmel as we follow these sequential stages of prayer:

6. For more on the distinctions of the three general types of prayer, namely, vocal prayer, meditation, and contemplation, see John Paul II, *Catechism*, 2697–724.

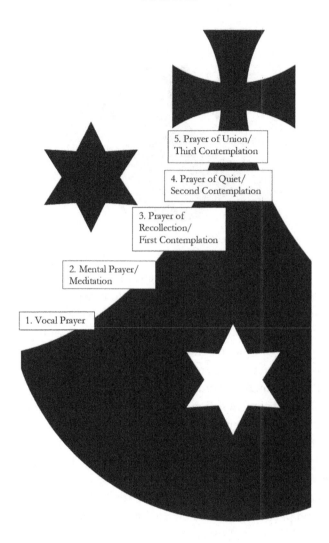

5. Prayer of Union/
Third Contemplation

4. Prayer of Quiet/
Second Contemplation

3. Prayer of
Recollection/
First Contemplation

2. Mental Prayer/
Meditation

1. Vocal Prayer

A. Vocal Prayer

Vocal prayer is the beginning of all Christian prayer, for it is the prayer of the church. Its heart is the eucharistic liturgy and it extends in and through the Liturgy of the Hours, devotions, and the entire repertoire of the church's living tradition of prayer and worship. Types of prayer such as the Rosary, communal Adoration and Benediction of the Blessed Sacrament, the Chaplet of Divine Mercy, the Stations of the Cross, novenas, and the treasury of indulgences all constitute what is meant by vocal prayer.[7] Spontaneous prayers also are included under the heading of vocal prayer.[8] This is the kind of prayer that we make individually or communally by addressing God out loud and allowing ourselves to be addressed by his voice alive in the church today through Scripture and Tradition, including all of the magisterial teachings of the church. Vocal prayer, while remaining an end in itself, is what "primes the pump" of the soul for the prayer of meditation and the prayer of contemplation. True meditation and contemplation cannot be reached aside from vocal prayer. Just like penitential practices, vocal prayer never will be left behind by those advanced in the spiritual life. Vocal prayer always functions as a warming of the soul toward union with God. Once again, the kataphatic movements of vocal prayer and mental prayer must precede the apophatic movement of contemplative prayer.

B. Mental Prayer or the Prayer of Meditation

The second stage of prayer is called mental prayer or the prayer of meditation. This kind of prayer makes use of discursive reasoning to ponder the mysteries of faith. The Holy Rosary is one of the best examples of mental prayer, as well as the practice of *lectio divina*, that is, a ruminate reading of Scripture rooted in the Benedictine monastic tradition of meditation. Ignatian spirituality, with its promotion of the full use of the sensate imagination (employing all five of the senses imaginatively) for meditation, is also helpful for understanding what is meant by mental prayer. The *Spiritual Exercises* of Saint Ignatius of Loyola are essential for every person who is serious about knowing how to go about mental prayer. The meditations provided in Saint Francis de Sales's *Introduction to the Devout Life* is another beautiful model for mental prayer. In the prayer of meditation,

7. The *Manual of Indulgences* is a tremendous resource for vocal prayer that is largely unknown by Catholics today. But those who are acquainted with it are granted greater access to the treasury of the Church's vocal prayer that has accumulated over the centuries of the Church's history.

8. Although Saint Teresa of Jesus has some stern words of caution about being too casual in spontaneous prayer. See Teresa of Ávila, *Interior Castle*, 1.7, 37–38: "A prayer in which a person is not aware of whom he is speaking to, what he is asking, who it is who is asking and of whom, I do not call prayer however much the lips move . . . . Those who have the habit of speaking before God's majesty as though they were speaking to a slave, without being careful to see how they are speaking, but saying whatever comes to their heads and whatever they have learned from saying at other times, in my opinion are not praying. Please God, may no Christian pray in this way."

through discursive reasoning, we ruminate upon scenes in the life of Jesus, other events of salvation history, or any of the mysteries of faith in order to be conformed more closely to Christ and the will of God the Father. Our devotion becomes more fervent, our piety flourishes, and our souls are nourished by the delectable fruits of divine revelation and right reason. The course of mental prayer composes the middle region of Mount Carmel where divine illumination happens: "For with you is the fountain of life, and in your light we see light" (Ps 36:10). Mental prayer moves a soul from the stage of a beginner to that of a proficient in the spiritual life. Similar to vocal prayer, even for those advanced in the spiritual life, meditation will continue to contribute to a soul's spiritual edification, even at the high altitudes of Mount Carmel.

C. The Prayer of Recollection

The third stage of prayer is called the prayer of recollection, and it is the first form of the prayer of contemplation proper. It is important to understand that contemplative prayer is the high-hanging fruit that is reached after the long, arduous, and disciplined practices of vocal prayer and mental prayer that cultivate habits of virtue in the soul. Contemplative prayer is both re-ward and responsibility. Above all, it is a gift given directly by God and in the Lord's timing. In most cases, however, it takes years (if not decades) for a person to experience the higher stages of contemplative prayer after having lived faithfully and consistently within the church's culture of vocal prayer and mental prayer. If a mountaineer embarks on climbing one of the most challenging mountains in the world, for example, Mount Everest or K2, he must do much research and training in order to climb the mountain in a safe and manageable way. He cannot climb such a mountain alone but must be accompanied by expert guides who have climbed the mountain before. He must climb the mountain not alone but with a community of climbers, each one trusting the others. Every climber must begin his ascent at the base of the mountain and pass through many intermediate camps or checkpoints on the way up. Certain conditions must be present to proceed up the face of the mountain at each stage, and it will take somewhere around two months to climb Mount Everest or K2. Most climbers need to use oxygen tanks in the high altitudes where it can be difficult to breathe. Once reaching the summit, climbers cannot stay for very long, but must descend the moun-tain carefully, since the descent often is more dangerous than the ascent.

For mountaineering in the spiritual life, we must harness ourselves to vocal prayer and mental prayer as we ascend toward contemplative prayer. Before becoming acclimatized to contemplative prayer, one must have become well acclimatized to vocal prayer and mental prayer. There is no other way, just as there is no other way to the summit of the mountain besides those well-established routes that best avoid avalanche and insurmountable formations of rock. You will harness at the base camp of vocal prayer and rest. You then will harness at the intermediate camp of mental prayer and rest. Spiritual mountaineering ascends one stage at a time in order to arrive at a very lofty summit that cannot be reached all at once. For Carmelite mountaineering, the third stage of the prayer of recollection is the most decisive, because it is the beginning of contemplation as contemplation.

Saint Teresa of Jesus's most precise definition of the prayer of recollection is found in *The Way of Perfection*: "This prayer is called 'recollection,' because the soul collects its potencies together and enters within itself to be with its God."[9] The Spanish noun *recogimiento* is derived from the verbs *coger* (to gather, get, touch, grasp, catch, hook, take, lift, grab, nab, land, accept) and *recoger* (to collect, pick up, gather, reap, harvest, glean, scoop up, bring in, rake in, lift, scavenge). The prayer of recollection is about gathering up the soul that has been scattered, diverted, and spread so thin across so many appetites, affections, and distractions from the *unum necessarium*, "the one thing necessary."[10] The prayer of recollection describes the process

---

9. Teresa of Ávila, *Way of Perfection*, in *Collected Works*, 2: 28.4: "*Llámase recogimiento, porque recoge el alma todas las potencias y se entra dentro de sí con Dios.*" The Spanish word *potencias* also could be translated as "powers" of the soul as well as "faculties" of the soul. Specifically, the faculties of the soul consist of the lower sense faculties that include the affective or emotional states as moved by the passions (joy, hope, fear, sorrow), and the higher faculties that include the intellect, the memory, and the will. Cf. 35.1: "*Heme alargado tanto en esto—aunque había hablado en la oración del recogimiento de lo mucho que importa este entrarnos a solas con Dios—por ser cosa tan importante.*" ("Because this matter is so important I have greatly enlarged upon it, even though in discussing the prayer of recollection I spoke of the significance of entering within ourselves to be alone with God.") It is necessary to combine these two passages of Saint Teresa to synthesize her definition of the prayer of recollection as one in which "the soul collects its potencies together and enters within itself to be alone with its God."

10. Cf. John Paul II, *Catechism*, 2711: "*Entering into contemplative prayer* is like entering into the Eucharistic liturgy: we 'gather up' the heart, recollect our whole being under the prompting of the Holy Spirit, abide in the dwelling place of the Lord which we are, awaken our faith in order to enter into the presence of him who awaits us. We let our masks fall and turn our hearts back to the Lord who loves us, so as to hand ourselves over to him as an offering to be purified and transformed."

of gathering up the fragments of the soul that have been scattered about over the course of earthly temporality. There are two phases to the prayer of recollection: (1) the active phase and (2) the passive phase. This distinction between active and passive is essential to understand the written works of both Saints Teresa of Jesus and John of the Cross. The first stage of contemplative prayer is active recollection. This stage surpasses that of all mental prayer, as it involves a real putting to sleep of the lower and higher faculties of the soul. The soul is personally and actively involved in freely surrendering all of its powers to divine control and mastery. Here the soul utters its final and lasting *fiat*—let it be done unto me!—before the face of divine gift. The soul relinquishes command of itself and yields absolutely to the sway of the Most Holy Trinity. Thereby the soul is stilled and hushed. All appetites and affections are quieted. All attachments are perfectly detached and disengaged. The soul is set free to contemplate God and God alone. Because completely recollected back together and re-membered, the soul is positioned to make its final ascent to the summit of Mount Carmel by letting itself be lifted by God as an infant in her mother's arms (see Ps 131). During the passive phase of the prayer of recollection, God is found to be doing everything in the soul and there is nothing left for the soul to do by its own powers, save for remaining open, dilated, and porous for the divine operations alone. This pure passivity marks the character of the two final stages of contemplative prayer: the prayer of quiet and the prayer of union.

What does the prayer of recollection have to do with gathering the memories of life in relation to the complete gathering up of the soul? Here we meet with yet another paradox of faith. Though the Carmelite Doctors do not go into great detail in response to this question, *The Story of a Soul* of Saint Thérèse of Lisieux is instructive. Of the three manuscripts that make up this work, the first and third are comprised of a recollection, or gathering up, of her life memories. This is a necessary kataphatic task before the apophatic holocaust (redemption rather than annihilation) of memories can take place. During the active phase of the prayer of recollection, memories from one's life may be gathered up for their greatest purpose in giving themselves as reasons to give thanks to God. When I actively gather up my life before the Lord, both through the examination of conscience and simply recalling "what marvels the Lord worked for us" (Ps 126:3), I gather it all up not as an end in itself (nor individual memories as ends in themselves), but as an offering to place into the hands of Jesus to offer in turn to the Father: "And it happened that, while he was with them at table, he took bread, said the blessing, broke it, and gave it to them. With that their eyes were opened and they recognized him" (Luke 24:30–31). In offering the recollected and remembered memories of our lives as an evening oblation to Jesus the Great Physician, everything assumes the potential to be healed, and everything assumes the potential to be part of the Father's plan to gather all of creation back into his bosom of fatherly care. This procedure is empowered by the anamnetic eucharistic liturgy of the church, in which we remember the saving works of God throughout the time of creation. The alleged idolatry and paralysis of memories is overcome insofar as these assorted memories of life are intermingled (as the intermingling of the eucharistic Body and Blood of Christ) with the memory of Jesus's paschal mystery as the apogee of salvation history.

The prayer of recollection is really the target prayer for the Carmelite. It is the beginning of contemplation and where the Wind of the Holy Spirit increases its velocity, so to speak. The prayer of recollection capitalizes on the self-exerting stages of purification and illumination that have preceded and prepared the way for contemplation. The prayer of recollection can be considered the target prayer for the Carmelite, because it is quite difficult to reach in itself. It certainly is not a given in the daily life of prayer. It presupposes that a soul is in no way stuck in the mire of sin, even venial sins of thought or omission. It presupposes that a soul is perfectly detached from all things of the world and that all unruly affections are in a maximal comatose state. It presupposes that even the higher faculties of the soul—the intellect, the memory, and the will—have become entirely recollected and are not given over to activities other than being totally immersed in this prayer. The prayer of recollection presupposes so much, and one cannot assume that this prayer is happening regularly, especially if all that it presupposes is not in place. All the same, divine grace makes it possible and desires that every soul makes progress toward this degree of prayer. While the prayer of recollection begins with its active phase—the soul working to gather up all of its powers fully in the direction of divinity—the passive phase of recollection begins the radical passivity of the soul that will characterize the subsequent prayer of quiet and prayer of union. With this transition to the passive stages of contemplative prayer, the Carmelite saints attest that vocal prayer and mental prayer can become more laborious and less productive at this time. Once the soul is swooning in the silent love of her divine Bridegroom, the stacking up of words can seem like a hindrance to the soul enraptured in the saturation of "the Love that had no beginning."[11]

D. The Prayer of Quiet

Following the passive stage of the prayer of recollection, the prayer of quiet commences subtly and inwardly. This is the genuine stage of supernatural or infused prayer that had begun to be ushered in by the passive prayer of recollection. In the prayer of quiet, all of the lower and higher faculties of the soul have been stilled and suspended, and the will especially is enraptured by the love of God. Though the intellect and memory may continue to roam a little, the will reins them in according to its immersive communion with divine Love, without itself being distracted from its attentiveness to divine Love. Whereas in the prayer of recollection, the soul had to do some of the work in gathering up itself and the things of God, in the prayer of quiet, God does all of the work: "the soul is like an infant that still nurses when at its mother's breast, and the mother without her babe's effort to suckle puts the milk in its mouth in order to give it delight" and "the delight is in the interior of the will."[12] In the prayer of quiet, all of the exterior directives of the soul are put to sleep, so that the interior senses can come to life while the exterior senses become inactive. Because the soul is so absorbed in the sweetness of divine Gift welling up from within the soul, all exterior former sweetnesses of the world become insipid, tasteless, and unattractive. The soul no longer notices such exterior attractions during the prayer of quiet. A holy peace is experienced that no earthly cares can destroy. "In the interior of the soul a sweetness is felt so great that the soul feels clearly the nearness of its Lord."[13] The presence of God is felt more than ever before in the prayer of quiet. It is here that mystical experiences tend to happen: locutions, visions, feelings of rapture or transport, flight of the spirit, spiritual delights and consolations, spiritual wounds, and such paranormal phenomena like levitation or bilocation. If any of these supernatural phenomena occur, it is due purely to divine initiative, and they cannot be willed directly by the soul; they are pure gifts from God. These paranormal experiences themselves are not the point, but they instead point to the point: the soul's closer proximity to perfect union with the Most Holy

11. Powers, *Selected Poetry*, 165.

12. Teresa of Ávila, *Way of Perfection*, in *Collected Works*, 2: 31.9–10, 157.

13. Teresa of Ávila, *Meditations on the Song of Songs*, in *Collected Works*, 2:4.2, 243.

Trinity. Saint Teresa describes this prayer as "that holy idleness of Mary," the sister of Lazarus, in which "the soul does not desire to move or to stir."[14] "All it wants is to love."[15] Even active ministry and acts of outward service are difficult to perform when a soul is in this state of prayer. Everything, body and soul, is occupied and absorbed positively and unconditionally in this contemplation and proximity to the divine Presence.

E. The Prayer of Union

Finally, the prayer of union, or spiritual marriage, is the summit of Mount Carmel and the terminal and crowning destination of all contemplative prayer in this life, for it is the threshold of heaven. The prayer of union is a renewed union with the cross of Christ, wherein the perfection of the interior life is unfolded in the perfection of the exterior expression of virtue and embodied acts of charity: "in this prayer it can also be Martha in such a way that it is as though engaged in both the active and contemplative life together."[16] In the prayer of union, Love is all. Divine Love surpasses the powers of the intellect and the memory and renders them dormant, so that the soul can love all the more: "Amen, amen, I say to you, when you were younger, you used to dress yourself and go where you wanted; but when you grow old, you will stretch out your hands, and someone else will dress you and lead you where you do not want to go" (John 21:18). And this is "the kind of death" by which the Carmelite "would glorify God" (John 21:19). Though the Carmelite soul would like to remain enveloped in the glorious cloud of Mount Tabor—the prayer of quiet—as if everything now has been accomplished, the Lord invites the soul to descend with him back into the valley to be a co-laborer with him in his vineyard of the world for which he laid down his life. A great paradox: the summit of Mount Carmel is at once its surrounding valley. The contemplative Carmelite apostolate is reinvigorated at the fringes, margins, and peripheries of humanity. Under the figure of the Incarnation, by which God took leave of his own divine solitude in order to woo his beloved to himself, the Carmelite recapitulates this incarnate movement by allowing his heart to be filled with all those faces and names who comprise the beloved of the divine Bridegroom. The universal Discalced Carmelite vocation reenters "to stand proxy for sinners

14. Teresa of Ávila, *Life*, in *Collected Works*, 1:17.4, 153.

15. Teresa of Ávila, *Spiritual Testimonies*, in *Collected Works*, 1:59.4, 426.

16. Teresa of Ávila, *Life*, in *Collected Works*, 1:17.4, 153–54.

through voluntary and joyous suffering, and to cooperate in the salvation of humankind," and to substitute oneself for the other for the sake of the other's ongoing conversion and resurrection.[17] Who would have thought that the prayer of union would be both solitary and missionary? Yet so it is. At times the Carmelite must take leave of his cell due to being "otherwise justly occupied,"[18] even if the Carmelite always will return to his cell as to his homeless home. Again, the Carmelite apostolate is essentially contemplation, but a contemplation that reaches out to the world through the loving strings and filaments of the heart. Missionary contemplation will exercise a perpetual service of the heart precisely through contemplative prayer, but also will serve with the exteriority of the body at a moment's notice when necessary.

For the soul that is lifted by the Lord into the prayer of union, "its love of God is boundless, for sometimes the love impels it so much that its lowly nature cannot endure the love. And since the soul sees that it is now growing weak and about to die, it says: *Sustain me with flowers; surround me with apples for I am dying with the sickness of love.*"[19] In her poem, "I Live without Living in Me," Saint Teresa of Jesus returns over and over to the refrain, "I die because I do not die."[20] The prayer of union causes a soul to grow more weary of living in this fallen world, "to go on living in the flesh," and, says with Saint Paul, "I long to depart from this life and be with Christ, for that is far better. Yet that I remain in the flesh is more necessary for your benefit" (Phil 1:22–24). There is no greater acquaintance of the soul with the cross of Christ than in the prayer of union. It is both sweet and bitter. However, over the course of time, the bitterness turns sweet in the light of resurrection glory and joy. "At the time, all discipline seems a cause not for joy but for pain, yet later it brings the peaceful fruit of righteousness to those who are trained by it. So strengthen your drooping hands and your weak knees. Make straight paths for your feet, that what is lame may not be dislocated but healed" (Heb 12:11–13). The process of the soul's thorough detachment of all created goods is a painful one: "Now those who belong to Christ Jesus have crucified their flesh with its passions and desires" (Gal 5:24). Responsibility for the other, when lived to the maximum degree,

17. Stein, *Self-Portrait in Letters (1916–1942)*, 128.

18. Albert of Jerusalem, *Carmelite Rule*.

19. Teresa of Ávila, *Meditations on the Song of Songs*, in *Collected Works*, 2: 6.12, 255. Italics in original.

20. Teresa of Ávila, *Poetry*, 1, in *Collected Works*, 3: 375–76.

is a self donated and sacrificed to the point of self-forgetfulness and self-abandonment, without remainder. To give in the cruciform pattern of Jesus is to give all, holding back nothing for the self. It is to arrive at the island called responsibility and to set all ships of voyage ablaze. But do not be afraid because *Deus dat incrementum* (God gives the increase).

III. METAPHORS OF CONTEMPLATION

In giving the increase, God approaches us with what is most commonplace. Jesus teaches us in parables that feature earthly and terrestrial goods to escort us toward even greater transcendent goods of which the kingdom of heaven is built. The Carmelite saints do likewise. They are inspired by visible goods of creation that serve as signs of the invisible mysteries of faith. For example, let us recall the three primary metaphors used by Saints Teresa of Jesus and John of the Cross to describe the patient progression of contemplative prayer. Saint Teresa of Jesus compares this spiritual progression to two related concrete images: (1) different types of water and (2) the soul as an interior castle that ventures into its innermost chambers. Saint John of the Cross, for his part, employs the grand metaphor of the dark night to guide us through the surprising movement of the soul up the steep slopes of Mount Carmel. It is difficult to understand the science of contemplation. Often it is much more straightforward to experience it than to talk about it. Like many mysteries of faith, metaphor is commonly the best approach to such mysteries that remain inaccessible directly by the five physical senses. Metaphors give us tangible images to work with through a sacramental imagination of spirit. The main metaphors of contemplation featured by Saints Teresa of Jesus and John of the Cross can be synthesized by mapping them onto the distinct stages of ascent from the diagram of Mount Carmel shown earlier in this chapter:

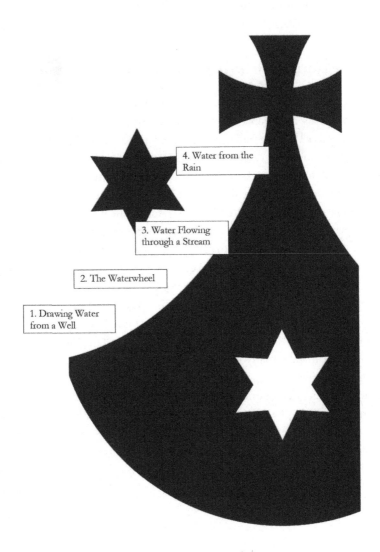

4. Water from the Rain

3. Water Flowing through a Stream

2. The Waterwheel

1. Drawing Water from a Well

The Four Different Types of Water

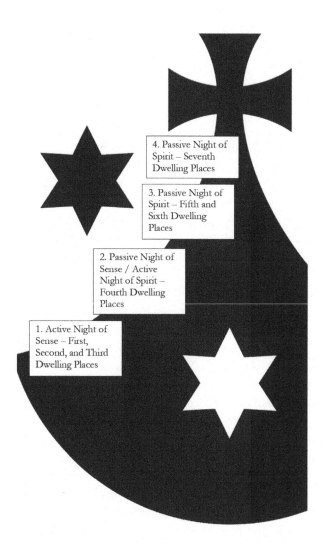

4. Passive Night of Spirit – Seventh Dwelling Places

3. Passive Night of Spirit – Fifth and Sixth Dwelling Places

2. Passive Night of Sense / Active Night of Spirit – Fourth Dwelling Places

1. Active Night of Sense – First, Second, and Third Dwelling Places

The Two Dark Nights of the Soul and the Seven Dwelling Places of the Interior Castle

| Stage 1: The active night of sense | Stage 2: The passive night of sense / The active night of spirit | Stages 3–4: The passive night of spirit |

The Two Dark Nights of the Soul

Now let us try briefly to make sense of the three preceding diagrams. The point here is only to suggest some general connections among the prime metaphors used by Saints Teresa of Ávila and John of the Cross in talking about the gradual stages of the contemplative life. For much more detail into these metaphors, we refer the reader to consult directly the writings of these Doctors of the church.[21] What we are trying to tie together are three independent metaphors into one spiritual ascent. Saint Teresa's metaphor of water has four different stages. Her metaphor of the interior castle has seven different stages. Saint John of the Cross's metaphor of the dark night has four stages, though there is some overlap of these, as shown in the diagram above. And so, the task we are setting for ourselves to conclude this chapter is to hint at how these diverse metaphors relate to the five levels of prayer discussed above. Vocal prayer and mental prayer correspond to the act of drawing water from a well; to the active night of sense; and to the first, second, and third dwelling places of the interior castle of the soul. The prayer of recollection, especially in its passive phase, corresponds to the waterwheel and the transition from the passive night of sense; to the active night of spirit; and to the fourth dwelling places of the interior castle of the soul. The prayer of quiet corresponds to the water flowing through a stream; to the beginning of the passive night of spirit; and to the fifth and sixth dwelling places of the interior castle of the soul. Finally, the prayer of union corresponds to the water from the rain; to the last stages of the

21. For more on the metaphor of water, see Teresa of Ávila, *Life*, in *Collected Works*, vol. 1. For more on the metaphor of the soul as an interior castle, see Teresa of Ávila, *Interior Castle*. For more on the metaphor of the dark night of the soul, see John of the Cross, *Ascent of Mount Carmel* and *Dark Night*.

passive night of spirit; and to the seventh dwelling places of the interior castle of the soul. Let us consider these metaphors in turn as they relate to one another and to the five types of prayer.

A. Drawing Water from a Well

In her autobiography, Saint Teresa of Jesus relies on the metaphor of water to tell about what is happening to the soul as it makes its ascent up Mount Carmel. One of Saint Teresa of Jesus's gifts as a writer is to help Carmelite spirituality be more comprehensible by making rather abstract theological concepts come down to earth. The first type of water is that from a well. This water is used to give drink to all of the flowers in the soul's spiritual garden, Carmel (garden of God). Beginners in the Carmelite path of prayer must be very active in developing habits of vocal prayer and mental prayer before proceeding to the active prayer of recollection. They also must practice regular examination of conscience and pondering their past life for the sake of deeper conversion. Drawing water from a well takes habitual effort and the first, second, and third dwelling places of the interior castle of the soul are unlocked and irrigated by this kind of water. Saint Teresa of Jesus even specifies this water as "tears . . . interior tenderness and feelings of devotion."[22] These are tears and feelings of compunction that bring about the purification necessary to continue the ascent up Mount Carmel. For his part, Saint John of the Cross speaks about the beginning of the active dark night of sense in *The Ascent of Mount Carmel*.[23] Why does he refer to this as a night? He gives us three reasons at the beginning of this work: "We can offer three reasons for calling this journey toward union with God a night. The first has to do with the point of departure, because individuals must deprive themselves of their appetites for worldly possessions. This denial and privation is like a night for all one's senses. The second reason refers to the means or the road along which a person travels to this union. Now this road is faith, and for the intellect faith is also like a dark night. The third reason pertains to the point of arrival, namely God. And God is also a dark night to the soul in this life. These three nights pass through a soul, or better, the soul passes through them in order to reach union with God."[24] So,

22. Teresa of Ávila, *Life*, in *Collected Works*, 1:11.9, 114.

23. For more details about the beginning of the dark night of sense, see John of the Cross, *Ascent of Mount Carmel*, I.13, 147–51.

24. John of the Cross, *Ascent of Mount Carmel*, I.2.1, 120.

all three of these metaphors—water, castle, and night—converge around the first two stages of prayer, namely, vocal prayer and mental prayer.

B. The Waterwheel

Second, Saint Teresa of Jesus talks about water obtained from a waterwheel: "by turning the crank of a water wheel and by aqueducts, the gardener obtains more water with less labor; and he can rest without having to work constantly . . . . Here the soul begins to be recollected and comes upon something supernatural because in no way can it acquire this prayer through any efforts it can make."[25] This is the beginning of the prayer of recollection, especially with reference to its passive phase. Once the crank of the waterwheel is turned and the wheel gains momentum by the force of gravity and the steady stream of cascaded water, the soul finds itself at rest with its God. Again, in the passive phase of the prayer of recollection (as well as in the prayer of quiet and the prayer of union to come), God is doing everything in the soul supernaturally. When the soul is perfectly recollected, the waters of divine grace begin to flood the soul like "surging waters" or "an unfailing stream" (Amos 5:24). Saint John of the Cross refers to this stage of prayer as the transition from the passive night of sense to the active night of spirit: "All natural ability is insufficient to produce the supernatural good that God alone infuses in the soul passively, secretly, and in silence. All the faculties must receive this infusion, and in order to do so they must be passive and not interfere through their own lowly activity and vile inclinations."[26] In the night of sense, all the lower faculties of the soul are emptied and suspended. In the night of spirit, the higher faculties of the soul undergo the same purgative procedure: the intellect is emptied by faith, the memory is emptied by hope, and the will is emptied by love. With the water derived from the waterwheel and the emergence of the dark night of spirit, the soul migrates further into the fourth dwelling places of the interior castle of the soul. Altogether, this movement constitutes spiritual illumination of the proficients in prayer. Contemplation proper has begun.

25. Teresa of Ávila, *Life*, in *Collected Works*, 1:14.1–2, 133–34.
26. John of the Cross, *Dark Night*, II.14.1, 429.

C. Water Flowing through a Stream

Third, Saint Teresa of Jesus makes an account of water flowing through a stream (or a river, or a spring) to reach the fifth and sixth dwelling places of the interior castle or garden of the soul: "The Lord so desires to help the gardener here that He Himself becomes practically the gardener and the one who does everything. This prayer is a sleep of the faculties: the faculties neither fail entirely to function nor understand how they function. The consolation, the sweetness, and the delight are incomparably greater than that experienced in the previous prayer . . . . This experience doesn't seem to me to be anything else than an almost complete death to all earthly things and an enjoyment of God."[27] When there is this entire sleep of the lower and higher faculties of the soul, the prayer of quiet begins. The soul is enraptured in delightful suspension and given over completely to the divine Gardener who is busy at work tending and mending his precious heaven on earth. In this prayer of quiet, "rivers of living water flow from within (the soul)" (John 7:38). For Saint John of the Cross, the passive night of spirit begins here: "The obscurity of the spirit is far more intense [than the obscurity of the senses] . . . . For however dark a night may be, some objects are still visible, but in total darkness nothing at all can be seen. In the night of sense there is yet some light, because the intellect and reason remain and suffer no blindness. But this spiritual night, which is faith, removes everything, both in the intellect and in the senses . . . . For the less a soul works with its own abilities, the more securely it proceeds because its progress in faith is greater."[28] At this point of the ascent of Mount Carmel, living waters begin to gush forth from the rock of the mountain itself.[29] Here we have reached the stage of those advanced in contemplative prayer.

D. Water from the Rain

Fourth and finally, Saint Teresa of Jesus portrays the highest heights of contemplative prayer, the prayer of union, as water from the rain falling from heaven "that in its abundance soaks and saturates the entire garden (of the soul)," in which the soul "feels with the most marvelous and gentlest

27. Teresa of Ávila, *Life*, in *Collected Works*, 1:16.1, 147–48.

28. John of the Cross, *Ascent of Mount Carmel*, II.1.3, 155.

29. See Exod 17:6: "I will be standing there in front of you on the rock in Horeb. Strike the rock, and the water will flow from it for the people to drink."

delight that everything is almost fading away through a kind of swoon in which breathing and all the bodily energies gradually fail . . . . In this way a person can and in fact does spend several hours in prayer . . . a continual martyrdom" in "the fire of the love of God."[30] Typically, this prayer of union, similar to the prayer of quiet, takes many years before awakening in the soul. Fidelity to the lower forms of prayer disposes a soul for readiness in the higher forms of prayer. With the heavenly rain upon the soul comes access to the most interior chamber of the soul's castle—the seventh dwelling places where Christ the King reigns. For Saint John of the Cross, the final phase of the passive dark night of spirit is the emptying of the human will by divine love: "The entire matter of reaching union with God consists in purging the will of its appetites and emotions so that from a human and lowly will it may be changed into the divine will, made identical with the will of God."[31] At this stage, the summit of Mount Carmel has been reached and therefore the soul once again "longs to depart this life and be with Christ, for that is far better" (Phil 1:23). Nevertheless, the Carmelite always will admit "that I remain in the flesh is more necessary for your benefit" (Phil 1:24).

> Elijah then said to Ahab, "Go up, eat and drink, for there is the sound of a heavy rain." So Ahab went up to eat and drink, while Elijah went up to the top of Carmel, crouched down to the earth, and put his head between his knees. He said to his servant, "Go up and look out to sea." He went up and looked, but reported, "There is nothing." Seven times he said, "Go look again!" And the seventh time the youth reported, "There is a cloud as small as a man's hand rising from the sea." Elijah said, "Go and say to Ahab, 'Harness up and go down the mountain before the rain stops you.'" All at once the sky grew dark with clouds and wind, and a heavy rain fell.
> 1 Kgs 18:41–45

---

30. Teresa of Ávila, *Life*, in *Collected Works*, 1:18.9–10, 13; 21.7; 161–62; 188.

31. John of the Cross, *Ascent of Mount Carmel*, III.16.3, 293.

Testimony

7

Our Testimony, Part I
Childhood

EMMANUEL MARY OF THE CROSS

WHEN ASKED BY A close friend how and why she converted to the Catholic faith, Edith Stein replied, "*Secretum meum mihi*" (My own secret for myself).[1] In a similar way, it is difficult to relate my gradual approach to Carmel. Altogether, it largely escapes my memory, and what fragments come into view are virtually impossible to put into words. Since Carmel is made up of intimate encounters with God, these experiences always saturate verbal expression and ultimately are a treasure to be kept secret as within an inner room with the door closed (Matt 5:6). Nevertheless, I will do my best to tell about what led me to Carmel and how my life changed once become a Carmelite.

As a child, I was drawn to quiet and solitude. Often an introvert of sorts, I would seek out secret and beautiful places to think, to dream, and, above all, to pray. I would talk with God about anything and everything. It seemed like all of my thoughts were thought with God alongside them, always in conversation with God. To this day, I believe with every fiber of my being that I can do nothing that escapes God's notice. It is the meaning of conscience, conviction, the absolute.[2] I sense God's presence as more

1. See Neyer, *Edith Stein*, 80; John of the Cross, *Sayings of Light and Love*, in *Collected Works*, 96, line 153; Isa 24:16 Vulgate.

2. See Ricoeur, "The Hermeneutics of Testimony" in *Essays on Biblical*

interior than my innermost self (Saint Augustine). I know God as incomparably merciful, but as incessantly demanding as well. The stakes of responsibility for the other are great, and no one can take my place as "my brother's keeper" (Gen 4:9). I have sensed this responsibility for the other as long as I can remember, even when I abandoned it in fear, selfishness, or cowardice.

Growing up immediately on the shoreline of Lake Michigan, I would go down to the beach often to seek my God. Enveloped in the breathtaking beauty of nature, I encountered God's majesty in the small and vast alike. Above all, I sensed God in my parents—in my mother and father—and in the haven of their love and security. Adopted through Catholic Family Services, six weeks after birth, from infancy onward I yearned to be claimed as a son—to be "rejoiced over with gladness" and to be "exulted over with loud singing as on a day of festival" (Zeph 3:17–18). One of my favorite baby pictures is of my Mom and Dad kissing me at the same time, one on each side of my face. For me, this was not only a picture of happiness, it was a sacrament of divine love.

While raised in the Catholic Church, attending a Catholic school from kindergarten to twelfth grade and attending Mass every Sunday, I was taught about God, the church, and the way of salvation. I believed what I was taught all along, and it all made sense to me. My young relationship with God was intimate, although hindered at times by the typical glitz and

Interpretation, 119–54.

glamor of worldly things. I acutely sensed that a rendezvous with destiny awaited and that this destiny would bring glory to God.

Four things were of highest importance in the Wallenfang household: our Catholic faith, academics, sports, and music. I was given the impression that if I excelled in these things, then everything would be all right. And so I did. As much as I was able, with as much strength and determination as I could muster, I exhausted myself every day in perfecting my skills and conquests in these areas. I became first chair trumpet in my high school band, starting quarterback on the varsity football team, and earned all A's on my report cards. My faith in God the Father's revelation through Jesus Christ and the Holy Spirit blossomed, yet oftentimes I would view God as a means to an end rather than the end—the point—in himself. I regarded God as the divine conductor who would make things happen according to my deepest desires, such as playing quarterback at the University of Notre Dame. However, I knew that God was calling me to turn over my life to him more and more.

There was a haunting prayer I learned in third grade that went like this: "O my God, tell me what you want me to do, and help me to do it." It haunted me because it was so demanding of my soul. To pray it honestly meant that I had to give up everything I wanted to do in order to seek God's will with wholehearted devotion. Everything that I desired had to be sacrificed unto God, so that I would be completely open to his summons. What if God wanted me to be a celibate priest? What if God wanted me to be a missionary? What if his will meant giving up football, trumpet playing, and that girl on whom I had a crush? It seemed too much. It seemed too difficult to trust that my life would flourish the most if I lived according to God's will alone. So I had trouble praying that prayer with sincerity. If I did pray it beside my bed at night, it was always with the provision that what God wanted me to do coincided with my overwhelming desires of football stardom and legendary greatness in all areas. "O my God, tell me what you want me to do, and help me to do it." This prayer would come full circle my freshman year of college, and it was then that I would pray it for the first time with every ounce of my being and with all sincerity.

VERONICA OF CHRIST THE BRIDEGROOM

Entering the Secular Discalced Carmelites was altogether unexpected; and still, entering the Secular Discalced Carmelites was perfectly expected.

Certainly, nothing from my past prepared me for my encounter with Christ through the Carmelites. Yet everything from my past prepared me for my encounter with Christ through the Carmelites. By God's grace, my past had enough rich soil to allow the seed of Christ to take root. At the same time, the soil of my life has been littered with enough rocks and thorns and weeds to rip out and discard. It is a soil that has needed compost ripened over time, fresh soil from other places, and the help of many hands for constant turning and reworking (Mark 4:1–9).

One of the earliest and most vivid memories I can recall is visiting my great-grandma Dee Dee in Northbrook, Illinois. She lived in a beautiful old home with a greenhouse attached right off of the kitchen. The greenhouse smelled so good—earthy and fresh—-and was filled with large green and flowering plants. A large wooden potting bench was always in use as some plant was being repotted. While the green house opened up into the most exquisite outdoor garden, the perimeter of the garden was lined with large bushes and mature trees. So secluded was it that it felt like a secret garden. Indeed, a garden enclosed. Even at a very young age, it was a place that sparked wonder and awe and was a place I loved just to be.

My Grandma Pat was also an avid gardener and over the years would share with me her love for gardening. She lived a couple of blocks down the street from us, and my sister and I would visit her often. All three of us would swing on her backyard garden swing and tell stories and laugh. She took so much joy in showing us what was coming up and how things were growing. She noticed all the little changes in the flowers: the small buds, the new growth on the leaves, and even the parts of the flowers that had died and needed to be removed. It all mattered to her.

This love of nature and quiet was shared by my parents as well. They delighted to take us on all sorts of outdoor adventures. Growing up in the Upper Peninsula of Michigan meant that there were more unexplored treasures of land than anyone could imagine. We would spend our days camping in forests, hiking on trails, scaling the sides of pristine waterfalls, and visiting abandoned towns from years long ago. My parents owned a forty-acre property that we called McFarland. It was a special place where they would dream of someday building a home and living a simple life. It was filled mostly with old pine trees, but there was one spot that opened into a meadow with gentle rolling hills. It was here that we usually would eat our picnic lunch, and it was here that my heart always felt warm. But that did not last forever. The dream to build a home no longer existed, and life changed, so the property was sold. My sister and I were getting older, and busier lives of school and work took over. The matriarchs and patriarchs in our extended family began to die. The stable foundation of life I had taken for granted now began to quake a bit under my feet.

Even more, something began to tell me that I should be someone I wasn't. Instead of clinging to the quiet, retreat-like environments that brought me joy as a child, I began to think that the noisy and confusing world had more to offer. Material things like money and clothes became very important. I would pride myself in having so many clothes that I would not repeat the same outfit for six weeks, and I kept a calendar to prove it. The tender relationship I had with my sister became one of annoyance. My parents were the last people with whom I wanted to be. And whenever we camped, all I could think about was how soon would it be over. More than anything, I just wanted to leave the secluded and oppressive confines of such a tiny Upper Michigan town and move to the big city of Chicago where life surely would be better. I had a life to live, and it did not have anything to do with what surrounded me.

Though the times felt dark and the path was not always well lit, sometimes a bright light would break through the clouds and I could see again. Like the summer weeks I spent at Lake Lundgren Bible Camp. I encountered Christ in profound ways: real-life-application preaching, skits, music, and challenges to read the Bible daily left me feeling like I was united fully to Christ. The experiences at the camp would linger long into the fall, giving me the hope and encouragement I needed to find quiet time to pray and to put life into the right perspective. And then the mountaintop experience would fade and I would be left again in the valley trying so hard to climb up the steep mountainside, but without the right equipment.

Just when it seemed hopeless, more light would break through. Like when I helped my Grandma Ellen serve food at a camp for children whose parents were in prison. I thought I had gone only to help my grandma prepare food, but instead she gave me a lesson in unconditional love. She knew exactly what the children needed, and it wasn't always the food we served. It was looking them in the eye, looking deep into their souls, and saying, "I care about you. You are loved." She would listen to them, hug them, laugh with them, and cry with them.

Other times the light came while I was playing music at a nursing home. Especially during the Advent and Christmas season, my sister and I would be asked to play the piano during a meal or for entertainment. The joy it brought to the residents would fill me up enough to last for days. In those experiences I knew that my life mattered and, in fact, I had a mission to help minister to other people in need.

The care and concern for others was fostered most definitely in my own family and also through my church community. Growing up, my family attended several different churches: Assembly of God, Mennonite, Presbyterian, Episcopal, Baptist, Church of God, and non-denominational churches. As different as each of these churches were, they fed me in a similar way: our God is a God of love who desires to have a relationship with us, and the community of believers encourages us to keep running the race (Phil 3:14).

Despite my own failings and self-positioned hurdles, there were many little seeds planted. Like gardeners who plant perennials, the first year is a time of sleep for the plant. There is little growth to be seen above ground, but underneath the plant begins to take root in its new environment and feeds on the richness of its soil. Perhaps this dormancy of a perennial is similar to a time of recollection. And perhaps for me these early years of my life were a time of soaking in all the richness of the soil of my environment in preparation for the next stage of the perennial life: creeping.

8

Our Testimony, Part II
Becoming Adults

EMMANUEL MARY OF THE CROSS

DURING THE SPRING OF my senior year of high school, I received a phone call from my close friend's father, Jim Muldoon. At the time, Jim was growing leaps and bounds in his faith and he wanted to meet with me one afternoon at Caffe Tosi in downtown Saint Joseph, Michigan. He wanted to talk. When we met that afternoon over coffee and hot chocolate, he told me that he had had a dream in which he saw me on stage in a rage—yelling and screaming and throwing things all over the place. He took it to be a warning sign that caused him concern. He was worried about me, that I was so set on playing quarterback at Notre Dame that I might have a severe crisis if this plan didn't work out.

Jim knew me well. He often trained with me in weight lifting and conditioning throughout high school. He was a great cheerleader, and he wanted to see me succeed. However, not only did he want me to be realistic about future possibilities, he wanted me to think about God's possibility for my life. So at this meeting, he continued to talk to me about the idea of God's will—that God had a definite plan for my life and that I should seek out this plan with all my heart.

He said to me, "Donny, your life is like a bucket, full of all these things you hope for and desire. But, in order to know God's will, you have to dump out your bucket completely, and then it will be perfectly empty for God to fill it with what he wants to be in it." This was a great revelation to me, and I remember walking away from that meeting pondering over this revolutionary concept of God's will.

Over time I took it to heart, and I became fully prepared for the day when the door to the land of the golden dome would close and the door to the field of dreams would open wide. I accepted a Presidential Scholarship to attend Albion College and play football and music there. My freshman year was tremendous. I was a pre-med major, football player, and trumpet player in several ensembles. I met many wonderful friends who were rooted in their Christian faith. I attended Catholic Mass and InterVarsity Christian Fellowship faithfully. At Christmas break I went to the Urbana missions conference, which catapulted me even further in my relationship with God. While at that conference, one of the speakers challenged us to read the entire Bible. I took her up on that challenge and began a one-year Bible-reading plan on January 1, 1997. I would wake up a little earlier to read from the Bible thirty minutes every morning. That year I finished reading through the whole Bible, and I was ready for God to work through me as his instrument to bring the world closer to him.

Yet even in the midst of a time of great spiritual growth, I experienced a significant crisis of faith that summer. "What if God isn't real after all," I began to wonder. There is a saying that goes, "If something sounds too good to be true, it probably is." Doubts started to creep into my mind and heart about God's existence. I was beginning to soar in my faith like never before, but my faith had to undergo a further test so that it would be even more genuine (1 Pet 1:7). Then one day a breakthrough occurred. I was sitting in the middle of my family's small flower garden—planted and maintained by Jim Muldoon—and I was overtaken by the beauty of these flowers. Peonies, rhododendrons, daisies, lilies, and so many other species—I was saturated by beauty and the glory to which these flowers gave witness. Their colors, patterns, fragrance, and delicacy testified to their divine Maker. This beauty does not enter into existence of its own accord out of sheer nothingness or out of an infinite expanse of atomic soup. It is intended. It is prophetic. It witnesses to an eternal flora and *paideia*—"a begetting in the beautiful."[1] I was convinced about God once again, then and there. I had to look no further than the flower, but in looking further, I was convinced all the more.

That summer I also went to visit my good friend Creagon Muldoon, Jim's son, in Sweden. Creagon was serving as a sixteen-year-old missionary

---

1. See Von Balthasar, *Truth of God*, 62.

with Kjell and Ann-Christine Karlsten of the Salvation Army Church in Visby on the island of Gotland. While staying there for over a week, we would pray often and deeply. During one of our prayer times, a woman felt that God was leading her to share Psalm 139 with me, as if God wanted to say something to me personally through this text. The climax of the Psalm reads like this:

> For you formed my inward parts, you knitted me together in my mother's womb. I praise you, for I am wondrously made. Wonderful are your works! You know me right well; my frame was not hidden from you, when I was being made in secret, intricately wrought in the depths of the earth. Your eyes beheld my unformed substance; in your book were written, every one of them, the days that were formed for me, when as yet there was none of them. How precious to me are your thoughts, O God! How vast is the sum of them! If I would count them, they are more than the sand. When I awake, I am still with you.[2]

Indeed, this psalm did speak to me. It spoke to me of my humble and hidden origin—in the womb of a mother whom I would meet only briefly in a labor and delivery room of a hospital, fatherless and motherless for a time in foster care, and graciously adopted at the threshold of forgetfulness. This psalm spoke of a destiny already known in the mind of God but to be unfolded patiently in time, space, and into eternity. It recognized the immense wonder and beauty of creation, the non-randomness of intentionality, and the symmetry of ordered randomness. It related the intimacy we are made to have with God and the common human vocation to praise his holy Name. At the end it featured a tremor of resurrection, awoken from sleep and remaining in communion with God.

At its essence, this psalm speaks of purpose. It attests to the meaningfulness of life and to the confidence a person can have in God's will and loving architecture for his or her life. My encounter with this text on that trip to visit Creagon in Sweden happened before my confrontation with atheism in all its seriousness. As a lighthouse on the shoreline of truth, this psalm would resurface during that dark time to remind me about who I really am as a child of God.

During my sophomore year at Albion College, Megan and I met each other for the first time. We were involved in the same Christian fellowship groups and music ensembles. We encouraged one another in our

2. Ps 139:13–18 RSV.

faith and oftentimes spent time together going for walks and stargazing at night. I offered to help her with her biology studies as she was working to understand DNA and RNA. She went through a tough time early during her freshman year as her parents became separated. This was very difficult for her, and I remember talking and praying through it at length. In spite of such hardships, I found Megan to be always joyful and filled with love. She was constantly solicitous—ever concerned about the needs and well-being of other people. She was involved in Best Buddies, an organization that connects college students with people with disabilities. Sometimes we would play music with one of her friends from Best Buddies. He would play the accordion, Megan would play the piano, and I would play the trumpet. Our friendship and life in Christ thrived during that time, and it blossomed into a divine vocation.

To make a long story short, Megan and I developed a deep friendship rooted in our mutual faith and were engaged on September 24, 1999. We entered into the covenant of marriage on May 27, 2000, at Saint Augustine Cathedral in Kalamazoo, Michigan. We both received bachelor's degrees in music and became involved in part-time church music and youth ministry while still in college. Upon completing our degrees, a door opened wide for me to become a full-time youth minister in my hometown of Saint Joseph, Michigan. For $23,000 a year, and with our first child, Ellen Agnes, born on April 30, 2001, our young family set sail for an adventure in parish ministry, surrounded by extended family and close friends.

All was going quite well until my father, John, was diagnosed with stage-four liver cancer in the fall of 2002. We were shocked. How could this vibrant man still in the prime of his life be dealt a fatal illness all of a sudden? My dad was even a member of my youth ministry core team. He gave of himself in so many ways, and he turned his disease into a platform to witness his faith to the local community. I recall him speaking at many Masses because he felt compelled to give witness to his faith and to make known the reason for his unwavering hope (see 1 Pet 3:15). A community college professor of thirty years in the field of political science, my father regarded his fate to be a political matter, that is, it concerned not only him, but the polis—the network of social relations in which he was enmeshed. It was as if he was more concerned about how other people were dealing with his cancer than how he himself was dealing with it. He worked hard to help plan his own funeral and to get things in order before he passed. My dad would go to be with the Lord on December 1, 2003, the Monday after Thanksgiving Day. My brother Mike and I were at each side of him the night he died in his home, after slipping off into a comatose state: "My dwelling, like a shepherd's tent, is struck down and borne away from me; you have folded up my life, like a weaver who severs me from the last thread" (Isa 38:12).

That very month I took a new ministry position at Saint Peter the Fisherman Parish in Two Rivers, Wisconsin. My father gave me his blessing to pursue that job the day he died. In the final conversation we had earlier that day, he said to me: "Clearly that's the better choice." Though I would be geographically further from my mother and brother, the sense of vocation whisked us away, and the communion of angels and saints kept us all bound together. While in Wisconsin, I went on to earn my master's in theological studies from Saint Norbert College. This opened the door for a wonderful ministry position at Holy Spirit Catholic Community in Naperville, Illinois, and enkindled my deepening thirst to study theology at the highest level.

After being in Naperville for not even a year, I sensed the Holy Spirit urging me to pursue something I had renounced in so many conversations before: a doctorate in theology. After going back and forth over and over with Megan and my mom, Linda, about the idea, I began to knock on the door of the doctoral program at Loyola University Chicago. In the eleventh hour, it opened wide and initiated me into a field of study that would open my eyes, ears, and heart to truth like never before: phenomenology. I was given the opportunity to study with one of the masters in the field, Jean-Luc Marion, from the Sorbonne in Paris. He took me under his wing, and I wrote my dissertation under his vigilant supervision and guidance. It was my training in the method of phenomenology that led me to the spiritual genius of the Carmelite way of life. More importantly, the experience of becoming a husband, a father, a youth minister, and a teacher led me to become a Carmelite. My wife, Megan, and our six children—Ellen Agnes, Aubin Augustine, Tobias Xavier, Callum Ignatius, Simeon Irenaeus, and Oliver Isidore—have taught me the meaning of becoming little all over again.

As each of our children was conceived and born, I was brought back to the place of contemplative wonder. I never tire of meditating on phenomena like the womb, infancy, and the majesty of littleness. Psalm 131 sums it up so well:

> O Lord, my heart is not lifted up, my eyes are not raised too high;
> I do not occupy myself with things too great and too marvelous for me.

But I have calmed and quieted my soul,
like a child quieted at its mother's breast;
like a child that is quieted is my soul.
O Israel, hope in the Lord from this time forth and for evermore.[3]

By pondering the continual outlook of wonder that my children show, I remain in wonder at God and his creation. Throughout my life I felt called to serve children, to be a shepherd to them, and to breathe life into them. As a father, I do breathe life into them, and they into me. They are an immense source of joy and consolation. Their goodness and beauty surpass all other natural marvels. To find God in a living, personal, and sacramental way, we must look no further than the child. The child reveals all of God's mystery in remaining ever so mysterious. Mystery unfolds mystery; mystery reveals more mystery. In her radical vulnerability, innocence, and docility, the child manifests and proclaims divine love and humility. John Paul II wrote poetically of the parental vocation:

And when they become "one flesh"
—that wondrous union—
on the horizon there appears the mystery of
fatherhood and motherhood.
—They return to the source of life within them.
—They return to the Beginning.
—Adam knew his wife
and she conceived and gave birth.
They know they have crossed the threshold
of the greatest responsibility![4]

Mystery and responsibility, fatherhood and motherhood—this is the Carmelite vocation. To be a shepherd of souls from the potent portico of ethical contemplation. As a father of six children, the threshold was crossed long ago. There is no turning back, and I must keep my hand to the plow (see Luke 9:62; 1 Cor 9:10). The souls of my children teach me what my soul is to become. Boomerang of grace, wherein the end is the beginning and the beginning is the end. "Amen, I say to you, unless you turn and become like children, you will not enter the kingdom of heaven. Whoever humbles himself like this child is the greatest in the kingdom of heaven. And whoever receives one child such as this in my name receives me" (Matt 18:3–5; cf. 19:14; Mark 10:15; Luke 18:17).

3. Ps 131:1–3 RSV.

4. John Paul II (pope), *Roman Triptych: Meditations*, 20–21.

The child is phenomenon par excellence, phenomenon of phenomena. For she signifies the call of the other that determines my perennial vocation to responsibility and thereby assumes the pride of place among all phenomena. Because of her, I am set free to love. Because of him, I attain to my raison d'être—my reason for being. Because of them, "by the grace of God I am what I am, and his grace to me has not been ineffective" (1 Cor 15:10). There is a beautiful song by the band Remedy Drive called "All Along." It speaks of "the world and its dreams" leaving the soul empty, as well as how all of our "castles in the sand" are washed away at some point.[5] This song speaks to me of my God and of my family. First, it attests to the fact that God is the only one for whom our souls yearn and for whom we have yearned all along. Nothing else compares: "I am the Lord, there is no other, there is no God besides me" (Isa 45:5). Second, this song reminds me that Megan and our children are the greatest gifts I have received in my life. They are greater than my job, greater than all my achievements, greater than this book. If nothing else, may this book testify to the supreme gift of the child at a time in history when children seem to be regarded more as curses than as blessings (see Pss 127, 128).

When desire gets restless, it often neglects to recognize that its goal has been granted already, perhaps even long, long ago. Greed is that vice which is never content with the gift. These song lyrics remind us that the gift has been given—forgiven (fore-given)—given in advance, and we have only to be at peace: "Not that I complain of want; for I have learned, in whatever state I am, to be content. I know how to be abased, and I know how to abound; in any and all circumstances I have learned the secret of facing plenty and hunger, abundance and want. I can do all things in him who strengthens me."[6]

VERONICA OF CHRIST THE BRIDEGROOM

Lacking a complete understanding of how to discern God's will, I began to form my own plan for how life was going to look: I would go to DePaul University in Chicago to study pre-med. This major would enable me to be well-situated to pursue a further degree in mortuary science at another institution. Indeed, I felt a strong interest in working as a funeral director. At the time I could not articulate with much precision what it was that

5. Ingram and Zach, "All Along."

6. Phil 4:11–13 RSV.

intrigued me, but looking back I can see that it was a profession that would allow me to help many people through what might be the most sorrowful time in a person's life.

But as God's will often happens, my plans turned upside down. The financial aid from DePaul just did not add up to what we needed. Completely out of the blue in the early spring of my senior year, I heard about a place called Albion College in Michigan. I decided to drive down to visit it for a night. "Something" was telling me to attend there. So in the fall of 1997, we drove my college necessities to Albion, Michigan, a small town in the middle of nowhere, so that I could attend Albion College, a liberal arts school with fewer than 1600 students. And somehow I was at peace with it all. A small sign of the beginnings of detachment.

I began to study courses in the pre-med major. But things were not clicking academically, and it felt like I was battling against myself. And yet I pressed on, trying to stay afloat in classes that were not speaking my language. Even worse, shortly after school began, my parents announced that their marriage was struggling and that they were separating. It was a devastating time in life. I had just left my family for what I thought would be a better life. And as much as I did not want them, I needed them even more. But it didn't feel like they were anywhere. I was wandering in the dark.

Yet in the middle of some of my darkest days a bright light broke through (Isa 9:2). By some miracle I began to become involved with InterVarsity Christian Fellowship, a ministry for college students. I was surrounded by people who loved Jesus, read the Bible, desired to live lives according to God's plan and purpose, and prayed for the courage to seek God's will in their lives. Ideas I had heard years before were being watered and brought to the light. And slowly, the fruit of these small seeds began to emerge.

This new growth within me inspired a passionate yes to all God had planned for me. And with that yes came a passionate no to things that stood in the way of my relationship with Christ. Detachment from the world came quickly and furiously. My wardrobe no longer mattered, nor did the car of which I had dreamed of getting once I graduated (a brand new VW Bug). I had no more concern of what my house looked like or what job I had or what town I lived in. I had only one concern: to do the will of God and to do it with passion.

During the fall of my freshman year at college, I met another student who had the same passion and mission in life. He and I spent hours studying

God's Word and in prayer, discerning where God was calling us individually. For me, part of this discernment led me to feel pulled in the direction of studying music as a major and the eventual possibility of entering the field of music therapy. It felt like a perfect fit to my restless wanderings and was the very mission field into which God was leading me. For my friend, he too discerned a music major, so we spent even more time together, now playing music (he on trumpet, I on piano). Our conversation in music blossomed into a conversation of love. Before long, our discernment of God's will became a united discernment, something that we discerned together. Was God calling us into a relationship that would lead to marriage?

Both separately and together, we spent hours in prayer. The answer was all too obvious: we were to be a total gift of self to each other and to join together in a marriage that would be fruitful and give life. Two and a half years from the fall that we met, Donny and I were married on a gloriously rainy day in the spring. Homegrown pansies and tulips decorated the ceremony and celebration, reminding all of us present that the life-giving force within these seeds and bulbs would burst forth new life that was flawless and fragrant and offered joy to all who beheld their beauty.

At age twenty-two (Donny) and age twenty (me), we were young, but had within us a clear mission and vision of what God was calling us to in our marriage. During the Easter Vigil, just four weeks before we were married, I was confirmed in the Catholic faith. Together we now shared and lived out a passion for the church's teaching on faith and morality. It inspired in us a new way to live: a life that clung to the Eucharist and was enveloped by the prayer of the church. Most mornings we would go to the cathedral church where we were married for Mass and to pray the Liturgy of the Hours. The Eucharist and prayer were what gave us the strength to live out our divinely appointed mission.

The fruit of our marriage that we so desperately desired was children. Ellen was born just one month before our one-year anniversary. Just as Ellen, our first child and only daughter, was entering the world, we learned from a good friend about the Catechesis of the Good Shepherd. Although Ellen was not yet old enough to participate, I began to search out what was so special about this Montessori-based style of faith formation. The retreat-like environment of preparation and formation as a catechist was a revolutionary time in my life. I soaked in everything and began to find myself yielding to the child and allowing myself to follow closely in this pathway carved out by the child. Indeed, a simple way, a little way.

In the atrium environments (places of prayer created for children to work with materials that lead them through meditation into contemplation), the children are presented specific works that aid in meditation on the life of Christ and the church. Without fail, these meditations move the child into a deep time of contemplation, where they remain very still and quiet. In privileged moments, the catechists get a glimpse into what the Lord is speaking to them. This may come through words they share or in their drawings. It was the Catechesis of the Good Shepherd that gave me adult language and understanding to the realness of contemplation that I had once known as a child: of being still, silent, waiting, listening, and peace—to the truth of my own place in the arms of Christ as a child of God.

We discerned early on in parenthood that we would homeschool our children. For us, this approach gave us the gift of time. Time to wonder. Time to linger. Time to enjoy. Time to do life together in all its beautiful mess. Cosmic education became family life, and family life became cosmic education, moments of the natural colliding with the supernatural. The time afforded us ample space for our children to settle into prayer, never hurried or forced. The time gave way to immersion experiences where we could be lost in new encounters and come out changed and transformed. The time also allowed our family life to be centered on justice and peace for other people.

As our family grew with the arrival of our son Aubin, so did our openness to the next chapters of life. We listened intently to where God was leading. And even in the middle of the sorrow and the loss of Donny's father, we were catapulted into a new mission. We moved to Wisconsin, where Donny would continue church work and pursue more education, this time in theology. It was in Wisconsin that our third child, Tobias, blessed our lives.

Just over two years later we relocated to the Chicago suburbs where Donny continued to work as a full-time youth minister. And as God designed, an opportunity for more education came. Donny began a PhD in theology. Of course, with the new job and the new house came another new baby. Callum was born. The seriousness of the PhD program left a desire in our hearts to move closer to Loyola, where Donny was schooling. So, we packed up again and moved into Chicago proper, in the Rogers Park neighborhood. Without fail, another child blessed our family. Simeon was born.

As the schoolwork was coming to an end and the dissertation process began, through prayer we discerned that we would leave Chicago and move to Michigan to live with Donny's mother, Linda. She had been diagnosed with cancer just weeks after his father, John. Her health was declining, and we knew this time with his mom would be filled with memories we would never forget. The year in Michigan was indeed an intense year waiting on the Lord to reveal where life was heading. Though often sick, Linda continued in her fight. Donny finished his dissertation in record time, and he applied for more than seventy jobs, with locations spanning from coast to coast. We spent hours wondering where God would have us. It was in the eleventh hour that the answer came. A Catholic liberal arts university in North Canton, Ohio, offered Donny a job that was too good to pass up.

For the twelfth time in eleven years of marriage we packed up our simple belongings and our children and moved to Ohio. Now the furthest we had ever been from either of our childhood homes, we found ourselves at home.

9

Our Testimony, Part III
Ascending Mount Carmel

EMMANUEL MARY OF THE CROSS

SO, WHAT IS PHENOMENOLOGY? This is one of my favorite questions to be asked. I think that I give a slightly different answer each time I am asked this question, and this time will be no exception. In order to relate it directly to Carmelite spirituality, I would say that phenomenology is a method of philosophy that leads to contemplation. How? Similar to the scientific method, phenomenology, literally the science of phenomena, proceeds along three basic steps:

(1) Bracket the natural attitude.
(2) Describe your experience of a given phenomenon.
(3) Contemplate.

The natural attitude refers to all the skeptical and cynical assumptions we bring to any and every experience. According to the natural attitude, possibility has limits, and it is up to me and people who think just like me to determine those limits.

Second, the natural attitude believes it impossible to have direct access to a given phenomenon. It regards each person's experience as distanced and removed from a given phenomenon, so much so that we can never get to the phenomenon itself, in itself.

For example, if we together eat a piece of chocolate cake, the natural attitude would say that you have your experience of eating the cake and I have mine. Our experiences are far removed from one another. You experience one thing, and I experience something else. Furthermore, it's only chocolate cake, after all, nothing particularly important, meaningful, or new. According to the natural attitude, "there is nothing new under the sun" (Eccl 1:9). However, if we approach the experience through phenomenology and bracket the natural attitude, everything begins to light up: "Mmmm! This cake is savory, delicious, and decadent. A revolution! As they say in Vienna, *Genuß*—enjoyment, pleasure, delight. Ah, the sweetness, the texture—how moist, how delicate, how soft and light! This cake reminds me of the German chocolate cake my parents always would get from the Bit of Swiss Pastry Shoppe on special occasions. They loved to eat that cake, and how I loved to eat it with them. How I miss them ... This brown chocolate cake reminds me, too, of the brown scapular of the Carmelites, vested in the mantle of Mary's virtue and maternal protection. This cake is sweet, but sweeter are the words of God: 'How sweet to my tongue is your promise, sweeter than honey to my mouth!'" (Ps 119:103). What a difference in experience—one shrouded in the natural attitude and the other liberated from it.

The fragmentary description of eating the chocolate cake is an example of the second step of phenomenology. One simply describes the experience as it happens with as much detail as possible. These descriptions are open to all meanings and aim at the most essential and meaningful parts of the experience.

Finally, the last step of phenomenology is to contemplate the experience. Contemplation opens the experience to the essence of the essence. It begins to move beyond words and even sense data. Contemplation yearns for the source before and behind all of this saturating givenness and desires to deliver a return gift of worship and thanksgiving. Contemplation crosses the threshold from philosophy into theology and discovers God who not only gives but reveals. Perhaps God is behind this experience of chocolate cake after all in such a way that my experience of God surpasses my experience of the chocolate cake to the degree that my spirit surpasses my senses.

Reenter the Carmelite way. Similar to phenomenology, the Carmelite approach to God first is concerned with bracketing the sensorial in order to give rise to the spiritual. All natural appetites and attachments must be divested and purged. There must be nothing left of them in order for the soul to ascend toward union with God. Like phenomenology, the first step is penitential and demands sacrifice. Everything must become nothing so that everything can become something and "so that God may be all in all" (1 Cor 15:28). All goods must be negated in order to approach the Good. All must be put to death—mortified—so that all can be redeemed and glorified. There is so much in common between phenomenology and Carmelite spirituality that a solid bridge can be formed between the two. It was this bridge that I observed to be at work in the life and work of Saint John Paul II. His writings collectively known as the "theology of the body" are the fruit of phenomenology and the Carmelite charism, approaching the mystery of God in and through the human body as sacrament. The work of Saint Edith Stein is similar in this regard, integrating phenomenological insights and Carmelite wisdom.

Interesting to note, it was Megan, not me, who took the initiative to find out if there was a local OCDS community in northeast Ohio. Based on our common love and devotion to the Carmelite saints and tradition, we began to seek out a new spiritual family. Sure enough, there was a vibrant OCDS community right up the road from us. Rosemarie Massaro, president of the community at the time, replied to Megan's email with haste and warmth. Ever since then, our OCDS journey began. Below is my letter to request admittance into the Secular Discalced Carmelites of the Holy Family.

August 25, 2013—Twenty-First Sunday in Ordinary Time

Rendezvous of Nocturnal Love

Dear Carmelite Community of the Holy Family,

It is with great joy and thanksgiving that I compose this short essay in testimony to my sincere desire to be incorporated into the Community of Secular Discalced Carmelites of the Holy Family. First, I thank you for how you have welcomed Megan, our children and me with fervent love to the monthly meetings and recent family picnic. Since January of this year we have felt the warmth and support of the community, especially in the wake of my mother, Linda's, passing into eternal life. Your prayers and concern were deeply appreciated and matched only by your witness to the spirit of Carmel.

To trace my attraction to the Carmelite charism, I begin by reflecting on my childhood. Adopted at six weeks old, I was raised in a Catholic home. My adoptive parents, John and Linda Wallenfang, brought me up in the faith through family prayer, the reading of Scripture, weekly Mass attendance, and sending me to a Catholic school from kindergarten to twelfth grade. They were supportive in all that I did and in who I was becoming. As a child, I was quite introspective and quiet. I regularly sought out quiet places to converse with God in deep intimacy. As I matured, especially through college, I read the entire Bible and came to a point at which I gave my entire life over to the will of God. This was a gradual process and, in fact, it is still unfolding.

One of the greatest stages of seeking God's will wholeheartedly was to marry Megan. In entering into the holy Sacrament of Marriage on May 27, 2000, not only was it a matter of seeking God's will on my own but it became a mission of accomplishing God's will together. It is this premise which has led both Megan and me to yearn for admission into the Carmelite community.

A year after Megan and I were married, I entered into full-time youth ministry in the Roman Catholic Church. Serving at three different parishes over the course of ten years, I have been living my life in service of the Gospel of Jesus Christ. My passion in life has become the task of sharing this Good News manifest and proclaimed in Christ to every member of his Bride to be, destined to enter into an eternal communion of love with him. This passion opened onto an unexpected turn in my life vocation: pursuing doctoral studies in theology at Loyola University Chicago. Much of my life has been a Cinderella story and entering into the PhD program at Loyola was no different. Neither was landing a position as Assistant Professor of Theology at Walsh University. The Lord has opened all doors along the way and has empowered me to listen to his bidding and to follow where he is leading.

I have been drawn to the Carmelite charism since my youth. There are several vague recollections, but one clear memory is how the story of Saint Edith Stein (Teresa Benedicta of the Cross) caught my attention. It always inspired me the way she was raised in a Jewish family, became atheist for several years, was initiated into the Catholic faith, and then died a martyr for the cause of truth and love. What appealed to me was her genuine thirst for truth and her relentlessness in groping for this truth. That was something we had in common and to this day she has continued to inspire me onward in the pursuit of truth. In addition to Saint Edith Stein, Saints Teresa of Jesus, John of the Cross, and Thérèse of Lisieux also have played a major role in drawing me to Carmel. I have taught Teresa's *Interior Castle* and Thérèse's *Story of a Soul* in my Christian spirituality course at Walsh. I also have finished reading the collected works of Saint John of the Cross and have been reading Brother Lawrence's *Practicing the Presence of God* recently. I have studied Edith Stein's collected works extensively and even have completed a book manuscript entitled *Human and Divine Being: A Study on the Theological Anthropology of Edith Stein*. On the whole, it was only natural to pursue admission into the Community of Secular Discalced Carmelites.

In studying these works of the Carmelite saints, I have come to realize the profound mystery of the human soul. To understand oneself as a created spiritual vessel of the Most Holy Trinity is one of the greatest and true realizations of being human. The vocation to enter the twofold dark night—as described in detail by Saint John of the Cross—is one that rings with such sober and life-giving truth that I can do no other than to say *fiat*—be it done unto me according to your word, O Lord. The cross, in its luminous darkness, has shown to me the meaning of life and the pattern of universal human vocation: to be a total gift of self and to be centered on the other rather than on the self. Jesus, Mary, and all the saints have demonstrated what it is to be human and what it is to be divine: radical kenosis, that is, self-emptying, to the point of abandonment. I desire to follow their lead, with the strength given by the Holy Spirit, and to make of my life a total gift without remainder. Carmel has emerged as a welcome pathway to this vocation which demands all and leaves nothing in reserve. The charism and community of Carmel run complementary to the general vocation of following Christ in and through the fold of the Catholic Church.

Entrance into Carmel has come at a crucial time in my life. My father, John, died of liver cancer on December 1, 2003, at age 56. My mother, Linda, died of the same disease on April 28, 2013, at age 65. It is almost like a second adoption. When I attended my first Carmelite meeting in January, I remember thinking that this was a community in which one feels at home even in death. Death is viewed as an initiation into the wedding feast of the Lamb. As Saint Teresa of Jesus would say, "I die because I do not die!" At this stage of my life I am at a crossroads where prayer wells up in me as my daily bread and life mission. Having five children, one is always on the run and serving within the context of the immediate family most of all. Prayer is a powerful and real way to serve others outside of the immediate family with constancy. For Carmelites, prayer is the primary life vocation. Prayer is approached with such intensity and passion that it leads to experiences of mystical transport and blissfully painful courtship with Christ the Bridegroom. It is this legacy of allegiance to Christ and zealous prayer which I want to hand on to my children: Ellen Agnes, Aubin Augustine, Tobias Xavier, Callum Ignatius, and Simeon Irenaeus. They are awesome gifts from God and lead me to become as a child in faithful relationship with the Good Shepherd.

In preparing to enter fully into the Carmelite community, I have been striving to participate faithfully in the daily prayers and discipline of silence of the Secular Discalced Carmelites. I have been praying Morning and Evening Prayer of the Liturgy of the Hours, attending Mass daily if possible, praying daily Marian devotions such as the Rosary and the Chaplet of the Infant of Prague, engaging in mental prayer for one half-hour per day, and examining my conscience every day. I also have attended regularly the monthly meetings and have gone to the Sacrament of Reconciliation on a consistent basis.

In reflecting for a significant time on what name I would like to request when being clothed with the Scapular and entering the novitiate, I would like to recommend the name:

Emmanuel Mary of the Cross

This name has much meaning for me. Emmanuel refers to Jesus, Son of God and Son of Mary, "God with us." It refers to the mystery of Christ's birth celebrated at Christmas, but even more to the mystery of his conception celebrated on the Feast of the Annunciation, March 25, for this is the beginning of his Incarnation in his Mother's virgin womb. Emmanuel also refers to one of my favorite philosophers, Emmanuel Levinas. His work runs very close to the Carmelite charism in its emphasis on self-emptying, responsibility for the other, and substituting oneself for the other. This is what Carmelites do when they pray with total devotion for the plight of the other. The name Mary of course refers to Mary, the Mother of God. It is her mantle of virtue which covers Carmel and I have placed myself under her maternal protection and guidance. Mary is the cardinal exemplar of a human soul completely open and docile to the influx of divine grace. Finally, the suffix "of the Cross" refers to both Saint John of the Cross and Saint Teresa Benedicta of the Cross. It signifies my desire to live according to the cruciform pattern of life-giving love. The symbol of the cross communicates the essence of salvation and divine love.

In formally entering the community of Carmel, I hope to contribute my God-given gifts to the good of the community. I hope for the community to be a place of nourishment for myself and for everyone who encounters me. I want to learn to serve authentically and to be shaped in the heart of the Carmelite charism: allegiance to Christ, humility, solitude, prayer, contemplation, fraternity, and intimacy with Christ the Bridegroom.

It is with this brief account of my life and my thirst for Carmel that I write to ask for permission to receive the Scapular this October. May I be found to be a worthy candidate in spite of my unworthiness of such an unspeakable invitation.

In Carmel,
Donald Lee Wallenfang

Since becoming members of the OCDS community, Megan and I have been showered with blessings. The number of these occasions are too many to recount, and the names and encounters with all of our brothers and sisters in Carmel are too numerous to mention. Nevertheless, one episode deserves special recollection. Our oldest children, Ellen and Aubin, became involved in a 4-H group and their interest in horses grew steadily. Over time, we discovered that horses are woven into the cultural fabric of Ohio as part of the heartland of the United States. Down the road from us lived the largest Amish community in the country. Some of our close friends had horses, and soon we came to realize that it was just a matter of time until we would have them as well.

Having horses was one of the furthest things from my mind: the cost, the hassle, the time commitment, let alone having no experience of taking care of horses, etc.! Even more serious, one of my good friends endured a tragic accident that left him paralyzed from the neck down while riding a horse. Again, another good friend's son had his horse fall on his leg and fractured his femur to the degree that he needed surgery to repair the injury. In spite of all this, Megan and I felt compelled to lean into the risk, the uncertainty, and the beauty of life, especially in and through its tragic fate. Derived from the Greek word *tragos* (he-goat), the term tragedy is based on the character of the he-goat that would represent the satyr instead of the more noble figure of the horse in ancient Greek satyr plays. The he-goat signifies a lowly, wanton, and ribald figure that accentuates the shocking nature of tragedy. Also closely related to the Greek verb *trogein* (to gnaw), tragedy gnaws at the soul and causes us to gnaw at an answer to its meaning. Tragedy forces us to ruminate on life like never before and to consider the possibility of a he-goat's metamorphosis into a horse. Tragedy results in catharsis—a process of purification that leads us beyond the static security of the material toward the dynamic circulation of the spiritual. Love is tried by suffering, and the resurrection comes in the wake of the cross. Fear would not be reason enough to deter us from these beautiful and majestic creatures which God created for human beings to ride upon and to take delight in. Though neither of us grew up on a farm, and the extent of our childhood pets were parakeets and goldfish, we were determined to pursue horsemanship as an essential part of our children's homeschool curriculum.

We ended up moving out into the country to a twelve-acre property with an old farmhouse built in 1916. This new home was a godsend that opened the door to the possibility of having horses. We wanted to live close to the land and to return to the dirt as the origin and meaning of our existence. Soon I made a call to our Carmelite sister, Patty Marvin, who said that she and her husband, Dennis, might have a horse they could give to us. That summer, Ellen, Aubin, and I went to the Marvin's Morgan horse farm at least once a week to learn all about horse care and riding and, above all, to muck the horse stalls. The Marvins were so generous to us, and they shared their heritage of horsemanship as a gift that would keep on giving. In the end, they gave us their stately and statuesque horse, Tenny—a nine-year-old honey bay Morgan gelding. We purchased one other horse, named Oscar, in addition to Tenny. Since then these horses have been a great blessing to our family and to all of our friends who have visited us over the years. Yes, we have brushed up against some minor tragic episodes, times when you hold your breath and pray with sudden urgency. In fact, I type this text with a healed broken ring finger on my right hand. It was fractured in two places when I grabbed Tenny's reigns from the ground as he had accelerated into a gallop with a terrified beginning rider on his back—an eleven-year-old girl—and he dragged me a few paces while she fell off gracefully to the side. Perhaps it prevented her from serious injury. Perhaps it even saved her life. For sure it reminded me that all is well that ends well and that eventual healing is victorious, ultimately through the resurrection of the body.

I conclude my reflection on being a Secular Discalced Carmelite by relating our adventure with horses to bring home the reality of the OCDS life. Our vocation does not come with the privilege of living in a cloistered monastery, even though our souls tend to live in such a way—silent, hidden, and serene in the fray. We live out this spirituality precisely amidst the mundane, the ordinary, the commonplace. My home is my monastery. However, it is a life in which everything lights up: the mundane becomes the celestial, the ordinary becomes the extraordinary, and the commonplace becomes the sacred. With divine grace, it is possible for he-goats to become celibate gelded stallions after all, without obliterating the meaningfulness of the low-ly he-goat. It is a paradoxical way of life. We are at once husbands, wives, and religious. We are at once fathers, mothers, abbots, and abbesses. We are at once hidden and exposed, lamenting and rejoicing, fasting and feasting. We are summoned to live the dark night of the soul in the noonday sun, to "pray without ceasing" (1 Thess 5:17) while surrounded by the diabolical urge to "cease without praying," and to choose only the "one thing necessary" (Luke 10:42) while being occupied with so many other things. The Carmelite life is exorbitant—everything is done with intensity and passion. Even silence is intensely tranquil, arcadian, and still. This life is exorbitant because God's love is exorbitant, spilling over in everything it does.

As Secular Discalced Carmelites, we return again and again to the concealed cell of our hearts to encounter our living God there: Father, Son, and Holy Spirit. We understand ourselves to be powerfully fragile dwelling places and conductors of divine Life and Presence that is not identical to our own finite created being. Divine Presence circulates through us in its constant influx, renewal, and dispensation. We aspire only to respire as spiritual vessels of divine mercy. We are the privileged wares (Latin: *mercis*) of the circuit of redemption, in our flesh "filling up what is lacking in the afflictions of Christ on behalf of his body, which is the church" (Col 1:24). We are the heart of the contemplative church, contemplating God not as a means to an end but as an end in himself. This kind of contemplative prayer demands all a person is and all one has to give. Contemplation is its own apostolate. Saint Elizabeth of the Trinity says as much when she writes that a contemplative's task is "to remain at the source . . . there are two words which sum up for me all holiness, all apostolate, union and love . . . (a Carmelite) must be apostolic: all her prayers, all her sacrifices tend to this!"[1] As Secular Discalced Carmelites, we bare the feet of our souls "to know God that he may be known."[2]

It is an austere, humble, and even rustic way of life. It is a vocation to self-forgetfulness and self-abnegation. Prayer ascends to the prerogatives of the other, substituting oneself for the other: "This is a fundamental premise of all religious life, above all of the life of Carmel, to stand proxy for sinners through voluntary and joyous suffering, and to cooperate in the salvation of humankind."[3] In a 1938 letter to Mother Petra Brüning, Edith Stein likewise

1. Elizabeth of the Trinity, *Letters*, in *Collected Works*, 2:191 and 2:136, respectively.

2. Washington Province, *OCDS Provincial Statutes*, II.25.

3. Stein, letter to Anneliese Lichtenberger, Dec. 26, 1932, in *Self-Portrait in Letters:*

writes, "I thought that those who recognized it as the cross of Christ had to take it upon themselves in the name of all."[4] This is the Carmelite way of life: like Moses, Esther, and Paul, to humbly and "confidently approach the throne of grace to receive mercy and to find grace for timely help" (Heb 4:16).[5] Carmelites take up the cross on behalf of the world through a life of steady penance and contemplative prayer that has the net effect of atonement. And as Secular Discalced Carmelites, we take up the cross embedded in the marketplace as its salt, leaven, and light, "until the whole batch of dough (is) leavened" (Luke 13:21).

VERONICA OF CHRIST THE BRIDEGROOM

Our life's journey that led us into Ohio was undoubtedly guided by the Holy Spirit. Certainly, all our experiences up to that moment had formed and prepared us for what lay ahead. Over the short years of our married life we had lived in so many places and met so many people. A sort of detachment from the world was the result of all the moving, and with it came a great peace to be anywhere at any time. We did not need any stuff to make us happy. Just to be, and be together, was all we needed. Perhaps one of the most convincing experiences was the loss of Donny's mother. Though wrought with pain and sorrow from her death and the death of Donny's father ten years earlier, our hearts were marked with a profound detachment from time and space. Our hunger was for the eternal realities that couldn't be conceived here on this earth.

For several years we sensed a calling to be a part of something greater than just our community as family. We were open to what the Lord would want but had no idea what would be his plan. During the last year of Donny's mother's life, we began to discern the possibility of entering a Secular or Third Order. Though all the charisms of all the religious orders are perfectly beautiful, it was more than obvious to which order we already belonged. Donny's passion for phenomenology had led him to the work of Edith Stein. He had a deep understanding of the dark night that John of the Cross revealed through poetry. I was not as well read but was attracted to the true feminism of which Edith Stein spoke and the little way of Thérèse of Lisieux.

1916–1942, 128.

4. Stein, *Self-Portrait in Letters: 1916–1942*, 295.

5. Cf. Exod 32:31–32; Esth C, D (LXX), 5:1–2; Rom 9:3.

Just months after Donny's mother's death, with another heavenly intercessor now praying for us, it felt as if we were catapulted again into a new mission: to join the Secular Order of Discalced Carmelites. We realized that we wanted the inheritance of spirit of the Carmelite Order—an order marked by humility, contemplation, voluntary suffering, and an intensified theology of childhood. Indeed, the roots of the Carmelites run deep, and as any large tree, the root system is as large and detailed as the visible tree extending into the sky. Spiritually, our roots were beginning to grow deeper and stronger, and we felt new life bursting forth. But this burst was quiet, without fanfare, and most certainly withdrawn. We had been pruned down to nothing, but it was this greater detachment that brought the most fruit (John 15). Definitely the beginning of our lives' perennial leap, but without much notice from the outside's eye. Hidden.

After living in Ohio for two years and with the discernment in joining the Carmelites, we began to prayerfully consider the possibility of finding a piece of land that might offer more quiet and opportunities for contemplation. The search was no doubt a spiritual journey. Leaving the city area of Canton meant that some of the ministries in which we were involved would change. But it was clear that our mission was one of prayer. Indeed, this mission held great responsibility: to pray for the world. Not just for ourselves or our family, but for everyone on this earth.

Following only a few months of searching, the most divinely inspired possibility came up: a simple home nestled in the woods. Rustic to be sure, and a fixer-upper to say the least, but a perfect answer to our prayer and a blessing for our family. Of course, to be true to the saying "new house, new job, new baby," we got a new house, Donny added another job to his long list (farmer), and we had another baby. Oliver Isidore arrived nine months after moving in!

For me, this home has allowed me to dive even deeper into the possibility of contemplation. We are surrounded by the beauty of nature: trees, birds, flowers, animals, water. It is indeed a garden enclosed (Song 4:12), our own Carmel. Our home, our little domestic church, has become our monastery. It is our hope that the landscape of our home and the landscape of our surroundings inspires in our children the same opportunity and desire for contemplation. In a practical way, we encourage our children to begin and end the day outside, watching the rising and setting of the sun, and to spend as much time outside as possible. Within our home, we have a dedicated prayer table and iconography throughout the house to help focus our hearts towards meditation. And on a regular basis we pray the Liturgy of the Hours together as a family, as well as *lectio divina*. It is this meditation on Scripture that really allows our children to listen to God's call and to respond to the questions "What did you hear? What might God be saying to you in this passage?"

Though there is a sense of busyness among our family with all the creative learning, laundry, cleaning, cooking, chores, and everyday living, we still strive to remain quiet. By this I mean, at peace. At rest. We try to leave our calendar as unmarked as possible. We let go of pressures from the world and seek only what the Lord desires for us. We set aside time to enjoy all the changes of the seasons: the growing and the dying of the natural world and of the supernatural world as well. There are of course interruptions in the rest and peace, but those are welcome encounters of grace as they beg us to give of ourselves even more. In fact, these interruptions, large or small, from within our family or from without, are the monastic bell to which we are attuned in empathetic attentiveness. It is the bell that calls us to come out of the cloister, through the cloister, and reenter the vineyard of the Lord.

May I close my personal testimony with the letter I composed on the occassion of making our first promises as Secular Discalced Carmelites.

Veronica of Christ the Bridegroom
First Promise Essay
April 12, 2015
Divine Mercy Sunday

Dear Carmelite Community of the Holy Family,

> *... and Veronica, with determination and passion,*
> *pushed through the crowd.*
> *She finally reached Jesus.*
> *In great tenderness and love,*
> *Veronica wiped the face of Jesus.*

Without inhibition or care, Veronica revealed her most desperate need: to be in the presence of Christ; to receive the love that only He could give. Like an infant, crying with only one desire: to be nursed by his mother; to receive the love that only she can give.

In the innocence of infancy, we grasp for the nourishment that our mother gives us, both in food and love. And so we are called to be a child of God. Like Veronica, we yearn to be held by Christ. This is especially what Thérèse experienced in contemplation.

It is this simple truth that I have only begun to comprehend that has illumined my prayer life. So often we work to have the "right" words to pray; we seek to have the "perfect" prayer. We think, certainly there is more to "do" than to just sit and be still. But ironically this is not what Jesus wants, and it is the child who shows us the perfect truth. It is ok to come before the Lord with nothing to offer but ourselves and to ask for nothing than just to be held and loved. It is ok to embrace the silence. This understanding of contemplation is the most profound growth I have experienced since the beginning of my call to Carmel.

I continue to be confident in my call to Carmel. In living out my vocation as a Secular Carmelite, I welcome the responsibility to pray for the Church and the world.

I am thankful for the members of the Order of Secular Discalced Carmelites. Their examples of humility and prayer are an immense encouragement. I only hope that my openness to spiritual transformation will help to lead others closer to Christ.

With the support of my family, I joyfully press on in this journey to live out the ecumenical councils, to receive the Sacraments, and to pray for the world through Liturgy of the Hours, the Rosary, meditation, and contemplation.

. . . and for that moment,
she gazed upon the face of Jesus,
and he gazed at her.

In Love and Thanksgiving,

Veronica of Christ the Bridegroom

(Megan Wallenfang)

Epilogue

JUST AS THE ORIGINAL Carmelite community was forced to migrate away
from Mount Carmel, Israel, to the island of Cyprus in 1238 due to political
unrest, the Wallenfang Carmelites were forced to migrate away from Union-
town, Ohio, to Harsens Island, Michigan, in 2019 due to spiritual unrest.
A new divine disturbance presented itself, and we interpreted all that was
happening as a surprising summons to follow the Master into uncharted
territory: "Rise, let us be on our way" (John 14:31).[1] Carmelite spirituality is
not meant to be static or to adhere to some status quo comfort zone. Like all
Christian discipleship, the Carmelite vocation is meant to be missionary in
nature: mission-oriented contemplation. It is ever important that the Carmelite way of life never serve as an excuse for unchecked egocentrism, self-
insulation, or a self-absorbed bourgeois lifestyle. As has been said before, the
gospel of Jesus comforts the afflicted and afflicts the comfortable.

Due to a variety of circumstances, we sensed a deeper call toward
missionary discipleship as Secular Discalced Carmelites. We desired
more encounters with the racial other, the religious other, the economic
other, the cultural other, and to be part of both an inward-facing and an

---

1. Cf. John 3:8: "The wind blows where it wills, and you can hear the sound it makes,
but you do not know where it comes from or where it goes; so it is with everyone who is
born of the Spirit." Luke 4:42–44: "At daybreak, Jesus left and went to a deserted place.
The crowds went looking for him, and when they came to him, they tried to prevent him
from leaving them. But he said to them, 'To the other towns also I must proclaim the
good news of the kingdom of God, because for this purpose I have been sent.' And he
was preaching in the synagogues of Judea." Acts 8:39–40: "When they came out of the
water, the Spirit of the Lord snatched Philip away, and the eunuch saw him no more, but
continued on his way rejoicing. Philip came to Azotus, and went about proclaiming the
good news to all the towns until he reached Caesarea." 2 Kgs 2:11–12: "As they walked on
still conversing, a fiery chariot and fiery horses came between the two of them, and Elijah
went up to heaven in a whirlwind, and Elisha saw it happen. He cried out, 'My father! My
father! Israel's chariot and steeds!' Then he saw him no longer."

outward-facing church community. We wanted to provide our children with an experience of the global church and not just a homogeneous encounter with more of the same. We wanted to participate in a community that lived according to a genuine Catholic dialogical openness to the world without reducing all things to the status quo of a myopic and prejudiced ideological worldview. We realized that life was more than getting tenure, becoming debt-free, and riding our horses around in circles while the rest of the world went on suffering. We prayerfully decided that the time had come for a change, and we made a plan to travel a bit further from our home every week to become part of a more urban church scene. On the very same day that we agreed on this new course of action, a door began to open for a new teaching position at Sacred Heart Major Seminary in Detroit, Michigan. A phrase that continued to well up in our hearts was: "We love your church, O Lord!"

The Lord confirmed this unexpected missionary territory with many signs in prayer and daily life. We ended up packing up all our belongings, leaving the horses behind, and moving to a new place where we had no friends or family nearby. We were moved to buy a house on an island, surrounded by the alluring clear blue waters of the Saint Clair River and Lake Saint Clair. Saint Clair and the Poor Clare nuns—those Franciscan contemplatives who witness to the power of missionary contemplation! Just as we were beginning to get settled into our new home, the COVID-19 pandemic hit, along with strict quarantining measures for the state of Michigan. With churches closed, we could not attend Mass for weeks. As Carmelites, at first, we thought that this was a fine scenario. We could be home all the time, secluded on this beautiful island like a hidden monastery, and have so much opportunity for contemplative prayer. There was some truth to this. But, as the days went on, we discovered what we were missing so desperately: fellowship, community, sociality. We longed for friendship and interaction with people outside of our nuclear family, and the viral pandemic was preventing such vital personal encounters.

Altogether, this was a revelation. Solitude is incomplete without community. There is a necessary complementarity between solitude and community rooted in the Most Holy Trinity. We were made for community and relationship. Silence and solitude are meant to cultivate the goodness of the communion of angels and saints in the intimate company of the Most Holy Trinity. Even the nuclear family—the domestic church—alone is insufficient unto itself. The domestic church is destined to overflow and spill out into the world. Secular Discalced Carmelites are appointed to be shoeless in the secular world, acting as an elixir within the world. Our individual human nature is bound up with humanity as an inherently relational reality: "'Here we have a splendid secret that shows us how to dream and to turn our life into a wonderful adventure. No one can face life in isolation . . . . We need a community that supports and helps us, in which we can help one another to keep looking ahead. How important it is to dream together . . . . By ourselves, we risk seeing mirages, things that are not there. Dreams, on the other hand, are built together.' Let us dream, then, as a single human family, as fellow travelers sharing the same flesh, as children of the same earth which is our common home, each of us bringing the richness of his or her beliefs and convictions, each of us with his or her own voice, brothers and sisters all."[2] A great revelation—that my flesh is not my own but is shared with my fellow human beings and intertwined within the natural order of creation!

In our postmodern milieu, there lurks the constant risk of separation, isolation, and alienation from one another. It is imperative that Carmelite spirituality not work to reinforce these dehumanizing trends. Instead, Carmelite contemplation is to be at the service of fraternity and sorority between the *communio* of human, angelic, and divine being. During the pandemic, we learned that solitude is meaningful and effective only in relation to community. Solitude without community is isolation and loneliness. A recluse is seduced to become obtuse without a deuce. In other words, it takes two to tango, and human nature is incomplete in individuality. Love cannot love alone: "Two are better than one: They get a good wage for their toil. If the one falls, the other will help the fallen one. But woe to the solitary person! If that one should fall, there is no other to help. So also, if two sleep together, they keep each other warm. How can one alone keep warm? Where one alone may be overcome, two together can resist. A three-ply cord is not easily broken" (Eccl 4:9–12). Again, Jesus says to us that "where two or three are gathered together in my name, there am I in the midst of them" (Matt 18:20). We all need more community, not less community. The psychological distress that accompanies a lack of in-person community is debilitating. Each individual's personal identity is formed in relation to other persons. Without community, no one of us knows who he or she is.

As Carmelites, the pandemic awakened us to the perennial fact that the final destination of the ascent of Mount Carmel is not a solitary summit

---

2. Francis (pope), *Fratelli tutti*, 8. Cf. 84.

but a liturgical synaxis. The liturgical assembly is the common apex of the spiritual life. The liturgical assembly is where the angels and saints gather in interpersonal fellowship with the Most Holy Trinity—where the angels and saints gather around the table of the Lord. This is the point. This is always the point. Solitude has power only in relation to this recurring rendezvous of eucharistic antiphonal encounter. Solitude is for the sake of liturgical gratitude and not the other way around. The liturgical tempo sets the pace for monastic mondiality. Carmelite solitude would be bankrupt without the liturgical communion of angels and saints oriented around the perichoretic life of the Most Holy Trinity. This liturgical orientation (*ad orientem, subsolanus*) prevents the Carmelite from becoming closed in on himself. As suggested in this book, Carmelite prayer is both inward-facing and outward-facing, both diastolic and systolic, both centripetal and centrifugal. Respiration is a twofold movement and so must be the life of the Carmelite soul. The Carmelite must do life with the poor and be taught by the poor. The Carmelite must be acclimated to both the back country and the front country. The Carmelite must be able to be at home in the wilderness as well as in the city. The Carmelite must remember the African proverb: "I am because we are; because we are, therefore I am." It is only according to this personal, familial, and communal standard that the monastic vocation has any meaning in the Church and in the world.

Emmanuel Mary of the Cross and Veronica of Christ the Bridegroom
Solemnity of Saint John of the Cross,
Priest and Doctor of the Church,
Father of the Order of Discalced Carmelites
December 14, 2020
Harsens Island, Michigan

Bibliography

Albert of Jerusalem. *Carmelite Rule of St. Albert*. Washington, DC: Washington Province OCDS, n.d. https://www.ocdswashprov.org/legislation.

Cannistrà, Saverio, et al. *General Definitory Letter No. 9*. June 18, 2011. In *Acta Ordinis Carmelitarum Discalceatorum* 56, 53. Rome: Curia Generalis OCD, 2011.

Congregation for the Doctrine of the Faith. *Placuit Deo*. Feb. 22, 2018. https://www.vatican.va/roman_curia/congregations/cfaith/documents/rc_con_cfaith_doc_20180222_placuit-deo_en.html.

Deeney, Aloysius. *Welcome to the Secular Order of Discalced Carmelites*. Washington, DC: ICS, 2009.

Doheny, William J. *Selected Writings of St. Teresa of Avila: A Synthesis of Her Writings*. Milwaukee: Bruce Publishing Co, 1950.

Elizabeth of the Trinity. *The Complete Works*. 2 vols. Translated by Aletheia Kane. Washington, DC: ICS, 1984.

Fitzgerald, Constance. "Passion in the Carmelite Tradition: Edith Stein." *Spiritus: A Journal of Christian Spirituality* 2, no. 2 (Fall 2002) 217–35.

Foley, Marc. *The Ascent of Mount Carmel, St. John of the Cross: Reflections*. Washington, DC: ICS, 2013.

Francis (pope). *Evangelii gaudium*. Nov. 24, 2013. http://www.vatican.va/content/francesco/en/apost_exhortations/documents/papa-francesco_esortazione-ap_20131124_evangelii-gaudium.html.

———. *Fratelli tutti*. Oct. 3, 2020. http://www.vatican.va/content/francesco/en/encyclicals/documents/papa-francesco_20201003_enciclica-fratelli-tutti.html.

———. *Gaudete et exsultate*. Mar. 19, 2018. http://www.vatican.va/content/francesco/en/apost_exhortations/documents/papa-francesco_esortazione-ap_20180319_gaudete-et-exsultate.html.

General Definitory of the Order of Discalced Carmelites. *Constitutions of Discalced Carmelite Secular Order*. Washington, DC: Washington Province OCDS, 2014. https://www.ocdswashprov.org/legislation.

Hallett, Nicky. "'So short a space of time': Early Modern Convent Chronology and Carmelite Spirituality." *Journal of Medieval and Early Modern Studies* 42, no. 3 (Fall 2012) 539–66.

Herbstrith, Waltraud. *Edith Stein: A Biography*. Translated by Bernard Bonowitz. San Francisco: Ignatius, 1992.

Houselander, Caryll. *Wood of the Cradle, Wood of the Cross: The Little Way of the Infant Jesus*. Manchester, NH: Sophia Institute, 1995.

Ignatius of Loyola. *Ignatius of Loyola: Spiritual Exercises and Other Works.* Edited by George E. Ganss. New York: Paulist Press, 1991.

Ingram, Jason David and David Zach. "All Along." Peermusic Publishing, Warner Chappell Music, 2009.

John of the Cross. *The Collected Works of St. John of the Cross.* Translated by Kieran Kavanaugh and Otilio Rodriguez. Washington, DC: ICS, 1991.

John Paul II (pope). *Catechism of the Catholic Church.* Vatican City: Libreria Editice Vaticana, 1993. https://www.vatican.va/archive/ENG0015/_INDEX.HTM.

———. *Roman Triptych: Meditations.* Translated by Jerzy Peterkiewicz. Washington, DC: USCCB, 2003.

Jotischky, Andrew. *The Carmelites and Antiquity: Mendicants and Their Pasts in the Middle Ages.* New York: Oxford University Press, 2002.

Lawrence of the Resurrection. *The Practice of the Presence of God.* Translated by John J. Delaney. New York: Image, 1977.

Levinas, Emmanuel. *Alterity and Transcendence.* Translated by Michael B. Smith. New York: Columbia University Press, 1999.

———. *Entre Nous: On Thinking of the Other.* Translated by Michael B. Smith and Barbara Harshav. New York: Columbia University Press, 1998.

———. *Ethics and Infinity: Conversations with Philippe Nemo.* Translated by Richard A. Cohen. Pittsburgh: Duquesne University Press, 1985.

———. *On Escape.* Translated by Bettina Bergo. Stanford, CA: Stanford University Press, 2003.

———. *Otherwise than Being or Beyond Essence.* Translated by Alphonso Lingis. Pittsburgh: Dusquesne University Press, 1981.

———. *Totality and Infinity: An Essay on Exteriority.* Translated by Alphonso Lingis. Pittsburgh: Duquesne University Press, 1969.

Liptak, Dolores. "Living the Carmelite Mission: 'Or, Rather of What Use Is Delphina?'" *American Catholic Studies* 125, no. 4 (Winter 2014) 89–113.

Marion, Jean-Luc. *Being Given: Toward a Phenomenology of Givenness.* Translated by Jeffrey L. Kosky. Stanford, CA: Stanford University Press, 2002.

———. *The Erotic Phenomenon.* Chicago: University of Chicago Press, 2007.

———. *God without Being: Hors-Texte.* Translated by Thomas A. Carlson. Chicago: University of Chicago Press, 1991.

———. *Negative Certainties.* Translated by Stephen E. Lewis. Chicago: University of Chicago Press, 2015.

———. "*La phénoménalité du sacrement: être et donation.*" *Communio* 157 (Sept.–Oct. 2001) 59–75.

———. *Prolegomena to Charity.* Translated by Stephen E. Lewis. New York: Fordham University Press, 2002.

———. *The Reason of the Gift.* Translated by Stephen E. Lewis. Charlottesville, VA: University of Virginia Press, 2011.

———. *The Visible and the Revealed.* Translated by Christina M. Gschwandtner. Perspectives in Continental Philosophy. New York: Fordham University Press, 2008.

Nancy, Jean-Luc. *Noli me tangere: On the Raising of the Body.* Translated by Sarah Clift, Pascale-Anne Brault, and Michael Naas. New York: Fordham University Press, 2008.

Neyer, Maria Amata. *Edith Stein: Her Life in Photos and Documents.* Translated by Waltraut Stein. Washington, DC: ICS, 1999.

Bibliography

Paul VI (pope). *The Liturgy of the Hours According to the Roman Rite*. Translated by the International Commission on English in the Liturgy. New York: Catholic, 1975.

Paul-Marie of the Cross. *Carmelite Spirituality in the Teresian Tradition*. Translated by Kathryn Sullivan. Washington, DC: ICS, 1997.

Payne, Steven. *The Carmelite Tradition*. Collegeville, MN: Liturgical Press, 2011.

————. *John of the Cross and the Cognitive Value of Mysticism: An Analysis of Sanjuanist Teaching and its Philosophical Implications for Contemporary Discussions of Mystical Experience*. Dordrecht, Neth.: Kluwer, 1990.

————. *Saint Thérèse of Lisieux: Doctor of the Universal Church*. New York: Alba House, 2002.

Payne, Steven, ed. *John of the Cross: Conferences and Essays by Members of the Institute of Carmelite Studies and Others*. Washington, DC: ICS, 1992.

Posselt, Teresia Renata. *Edith Stein: Eine Grosse Frau unseres Jahrhunderts*. 9th ed. Freiburg, Germ.: Herder, 1963.

————. *Edith Stein: The Life of a Philosopher and Carmelite*. Edited by Susanne M. Batzdorff, Josephine Koeppel, and John Sullivan. Washington, DC: ICS, 2005.

Powers, Jessica. *The Selected Poetry of Jessica Powers*. Edited by Regina Siegfried and Robert F. Morneau. Washington, DC: ICS, 1999.

Pseudo-Dionysius. *The Complete Works*. Translated by Colm Lubheid. New York: Paulist Press, 1987.

Rahner, Karl. *Further Theology of the Spiritual Life 1*. Vol. 7 of *Theological Investigations*. Translated by David Bourke. New York: Herder & Herder, 1971.

————. *Further Theology of the Spiritual Life 2*. Vol. 8 of *Theological Investigations*. Translated by David Bourke. New York: Herder & Herder, 1971.

Ribot, Felip. *The Ten Books on the Way of Life and Great Deeds of the Carmelites*. Translated by Richard Copsey. Kent, UK: Saint Albert's, 2005.

Ricoeur, Paul. *Essays on Biblical Hermeneutics*. Edited by Lewis S. Mudge. Philadelphia: Fortress, 1980.

Smet, Joaquin. *Los Carmelitas: Historia de la Orden del Carmel, I–IV*. Translated by Antonio Ruiz Molina. Madrid: Biblioteca de Autores Cristianos, 1987.

Staring, Adrianus, ed. *Medieval Carmelite Heritage: Early Reflections on the Nature of the Order*. Rome: Institutum Carmelitanum, 1989.

Stegge, Pius Aan de. *A Passion Flower of Carmel*. Translated by Joachim Smet. Chicago: Carmelite Press, 1940.

Stein, Edith. *Der Aufbau der Menschlichen Person*. Freiburg, Germ.: Herder, 1994.

————. *Essays on Woman*. Translated by Freda Mary Oben. Washington, DC: ICS, 1996.

————. *La Estructura de la Persona Humana*. Translated by José Mardomingo. Madrid: Biblioteca de Autores Cristianos, 1998.

————. *Finite and Eternal Being: An Attempt at an Ascent to the Meaning of Being*. Translated by Kurt F. Reinhardt. Washington, DC: ICS, 2002.

————. *The Hidden Life: Hagiographic Essays, Meditations, Spiritual Texts*. Translated by Waltraut Stein. Washington, DC: ICS, 1992.

————. *Knowledge and Faith*. Translated by Walter Redmond. Washington, DC: ICS, 2000.

————. *Life in a Jewish Family*. Translated by Josephine Koeppel. Washington, DC: ICS, 1986.

————. *On the Problem of Empathy*. Translated by Waltraut Stein. Washington, DC: ICS, 1989.

————. *Philosophy of Psychology and the Humanities.* Translated by Mary Catherine Baseheart and Marianne Sawicki. Washington, DC: ICS, 2000.

————. *Potency and Act: Studies toward a Philosophy of Being.* Translated by Walter Redmond. Washington, DC: ICS, 2009.

————. *The Science of the Cross.* Translated by Josephine Koeppel. Washington, DC: ICS, 2002.

————. *The Science of the Cross: A Study of St. John of the Cross.* Edited by L. Gelber and Romaeus Leuven, translated by Hilda Graef. London: Burns & Oates, 1960.

————. *Self-Portrait in Letters: 1916–1942.* Edited by L. Gelber and Romaeus Leuven, translated by Josephine Koeppel. Washington, DC: ICS, 1993.

————. *Self-Portrait in Letters: Letters to Roman Ingarden.* Translated by Hugh Candler Hunt. Washington, DC: ICS, 2014.

————. *Was ist der Mensch?: Theologische Anthropologie.* Freiburg, Germ.: Herder, 2005.

————. *Welt und Person: Beitrag zum Christlichen Wahrheitsstreben.* Freiburg, Germ.: Herder, 1962.

Sullivan, John, ed. *Holiness Befits Your House: Documentation on the Canonization of Edith Stein.* Washington, DC: ICS, 2000.

Teresa of Ávila. *The Collected Letters of St. Teresa of Avila.* 2 vols. Translated by Kieran Kavanaugh and Otilio Rodriguez. Washington, DC: ICS, 2001–07.

————. *The Collected Works of Saint Teresa of Avila.* 3 vols. Translated by Kieran Kananaugh and Otilio Rodriguez. Washington, DC: ICS, 1976–85.

————. *The Interior Castle: Study Edition.* Translated by Kieran Kavanaugh and Otilio Rodriguez. Washington, DC: ICS, 2010.

————. *Obras Completas: Edicion Manual.* Transcription by Efren de la Madre de Dios and Otger Steggink. Madrid: Biblioteca de Autores Cristianos, 1967.

Thérèse of Lisieux. *Letters of St. Thérèse of Lisieux.* 2 vols. Translated by John Clarke. Washington, DC: ICS, 1982, 1988.

————. *The Poetry of Saint Thérèse of Lisieux.* Translated by Donald Kinney. Washington, DC: ICS, 1996.

————. *Story of a Soul: The Autobiography of St. Thérèse of Lisieux.* 3rd ed. Translated by John Clarke. Washington, DC: ICS, 1996.

Von Balthasar, Hans Urs. *Truth of God.* Vol. 2 of *Theo-Logic.* Translated by Adrian J. Walker. San Francisco: Ignatius, 2004.

————. *Two Sisters in the Spirit: Thérèse of Lisieux and Elizabeth of the Trinity.* Translated by Donald Nichols, Anne Elizabeth Englund, and Dennis Martin. San Francisco: Ignatius Press, 1992.

Wallenfang, Donald. "Awaken, O Spirit: The Vocation of Becoming in the Work of Edith Stein." *Logos: A Journal of Catholic Thought and Culture* 15, no. 4 (Fall 2012) 57–74.

————. "*Cor quietum*: Saint Augustine and Saint Teresa of Ávila on the New Evangelization." In *Motown Evangelization: Sharing the Gospel of Jesus in a Detroit Style,* edited by John C. Cavadini and Donald Wallenfang. Eugene, OR: Pickwick, forthcoming.

————. *Dialectical Anatomy of the Eucharist: An Étude in Phenomenology.* Eugene, OR: Cascade, 2017.

————. *Emmanuel: Levinas and Variations on God with Us.* Eugene, OR: Cascade, forthcoming.

————. "Figures and Forms of Ultimacy: Manifestation and Proclamation as Paradigms of the Sacred." *International Journal of Religion in Spirituality and Society* 1, no. 3 (2011) 109–14.

————. "From Albert Einstein to Edith Stein: Understanding the Resurrection of the Body vis-à-vis Natural Science." In *Sixty Years after Albert Einstein (1879–1955)*, edited by Charles Tandy, 209–44. Death and Anti-Death 13. Ann Arbor, MI: Ria University Press, 2016.

————. "*Geisteswissenschaft*: Edith Stein's Phenomenological Sketch of the Essence of Spirit." In *Intersubjectivity, Humanity, Being: Edith Stein's Phenomenology and Christian Philosophy*, edited by Mette Lebech and John Haydn Gurmin, 499–524. Bern, Switz.: Peter Lang, 2015.

————. "The Heart of the Matter: Edith Stein on the Substance of the Soul." *Logos: A Journal of Catholic Thought and Culture* 17, no. 3 (Summer 2014) 118–42.

————. *Human and Divine Being: A Study on the Theological Anthropology of Edith Stein*. Eugene, OR: Cascade, 2017.

————. *iGod: A Hidden and Fragmented Autobiography*. Eugene, OR: Cascade, forthcoming.

————. *Metaphysics: A Basic Introduction in a Christian Key*. Eugene, OR: Cascade, 2019.

————. *Phenomenology: A Basic Introduction in the Light of Jesus Christ*. Eugene, OR: Cascade, 2019.

————. "Soul Power: Edith Stein's Meta-Phenomenological Construction of the Human Soul." In *Edith Stein: Women, Social-Political Philosophy, Theology, Metaphysics and Public History: New Approaches and Applications*, edited by Antonio Calcagno, 167–80. Boston Studies in Philosophy, Religion and Public Life 4. Dordrecht, Neth.: Springer, 2016.

————. *Trilectic of Testimony: A Phenomenological Construal of the Eucharist as Manifestation-Proclamation-Attestation*. Ann Arbor, MI: ProQuest, 2011.

Washington Province of the Immaculate Heart of Mary. *OCDS Provincial Statutes for the Washington Province of the Immaculate Heart of Mary*. Washington, DC: Washington Province OCDS, 2015. https://www.ocdswashprov.org/legislation.

Zimmerman, Benedict. *The Praise of Glory: Reminiscences of Sister Elizabeth of the Trinity, a Carmelite Nun of Dijon, 1901–1906*. Translated by the Benedictines of Stanbrook. Westminster, MD: Newman Press, 1962.

Index

Index

Made in the USA
Monee, IL
03 December 2021

83810392R00085